SOURCES

1. Originally published in The Complete Story of Passover (Merkos Publications).
2. See Likutei Sichot, vol. 11, p. 21. Ramban, Exodus 6:6-7.
3. Rashi, Pesachim 114a. Shulchan Aruch Harav 473:14.
4. Talmud, Pesachim 115b.
5. Haggadah Shel Pesach Im Likutei Taamim, Minhagim Ubiurim.
6. Haggadah Shel Pesach Im Likutei Taamim, Minhagim Ubiurim. Shulchan Aruch Harav 475:5, 7.
7. Haggadah Shel Pesach Im Likutei Taamim, Minhagim Ubiurim.
8. Likutei Sichot, vol. 17, p. 78.
9. Haggadah Shel Pesach Im Likutei Taamim, Minhagim Ubiurim.
10. Based on Haggadah Shel Pesach Im Likutei Taamim, Minhagim Ubiurim.
11. Ritva, Rid, Orchot Chaim, and others.
12. Likutei Sichot, vol. 1, p. 244.
13. Haggadah Shel Pesach Im Likutei Taamim, Minhagim Ubiurim.
14. Shibolei Haleket.
15. Bereishit Rabbah 68:9.
16. See Zevach Pesach (Abarbanel).
17. See letter printed at the beginning of this Haggadah. Also, Likutei Sichot, vol. 17, p. 264.
18. Talk of the Rebbe, second night of Passover, 5725 (1965) (Haggadah Im Biurim, p. 139).
19. Zevach Pesach (Abarbanel).
20. Maamar Ki Yishalcha Bincha 5738.
21. R. Tzadok HaKohen, Haggadah. Likutei Sichot, vol. 1, p. 247, and vol. 11, p. 2.
22. Gevurot Hashem (Maharal), chapter 67.
23. Talk of the Rebbe, second night of Passover 5725 (1965) (Haggadah Im Biurim, p. 139).
24. Zevach Pesach (Abarbanel). Maaseh Nissim (R. Yaakov of Lisa). See, however, Abudraham.
25. Public letter from the Rebbe for Passover 5717 (1957).
26. Maimonides, Hilchot Avodah Zarah, chapter 1.
27. Chovot Halevavot, sha'ar 2, chapter 5. Yain Malchut, p. 68.
28. Rashi.
29. Targum Onkelos.
30. Abudraham.
31. Rashi. Metzudot David. Shibolei Haleket.
32. Shnei Luchot HaBrit, Mesechet Pesachim, derush 5.
33. Public letter from the Rebbe for Passover 5718 (1958) (Haggadah Shel Pesach Im Likutei Taamim, Minhagum Ubiurim, p. 583).
34. Likutei Sichot, vol. 6, p. 13.
35. Rashi. Ramban. Rabeinu Bachye. Torah Ohr, Vayera 15b.
36. Shibolei Haleket.
37. See Pri Eitz Chaim, Birkat Hamazon.
38. Likutei Sichot, vol. 38, p. 184.
39. See Likutei Sichot, vol. 16, p. 87.
40. Zevach Pesach (Abarbanel).
41. Likutei Sichot, vol. 17, p. 78.
42. Tanya, chapters 31 and 36.
43. Tanya, chapter 47. Maharal, Gevurot Hashem, chapter 61.
44. Likutei Sichot, vol. 4, p. 1298.
45. Talmud, Pesachim 118b.
46. Alshich.
47. Proverbs 31:10-31.
48. Psalms 23.
49. This is a Kabbalistic term for a manifestation of the Divine Presence.
50. Zohar II:88a-b.

Hamotzi

Pour water on each hand three times using a washing cup, covering the entire hand each time, from the wrist to the fingertips, and say:

בָּרוּךְ אַתָּה יְיָ, אֱלֹהֵינוּ מֶלֶךְ הָעוֹלָם, אֲשֶׁר קִדְּשָׁנוּ בְּמִצְוֹתָיו, וְצִוָּנוּ עַל נְטִילַת יָדָיִם:

BLESSED are You, God, our God, King of the universe, who has made us holy with His mitzvahs, and commanded us concerning washing hands.

The head of the household recites the blessing for bread while holding two matzahs.

בָּרוּךְ אַתָּה יְיָ, אֱלֹהֵינוּ מֶלֶךְ הָעוֹלָם, הַמּוֹצִיא לֶחֶם מִן הָאָרֶץ:

BLESSED are You, God our God, King of the universe, who brings forth bread from the earth.

Distribute a piece to each person, who in turn recites the above blessing before eating.

IF you restrain your feet because of the Shabbat from attending to your affairs on My holy day, and you call the Shabbat "delight," the day made holy by God "honored," and you honor it by not following your customary ways, refraining from pursuing your affairs and from speaking profane things, then you shall delight in God, and I will make you ride on the high places of the earth, and I will nourish you with the heritage of Jacob your father; thus the mouth of God has spoken.

THIS is the meal of the holy Ancient One.

REMEMBER the Shabbat day to sanctify it. Six days you shall labor and do all your work, but the seventh day is Shabbat for God your God; you shall not do any work—you, your son or your daughter, your manservant or your maidservant, or your cattle, or the stranger within your gates. For [in] six days God made the heavens, the earth, the sea, and all that is in them, and rested on the seventh day—

 Lift the cup and hold it in the palm of your right hand, and say:

Therefore God blessed the Shabbat day and made it holy.

THESE are the festivals of God, holy assemblies, which you shall proclaim at their appointed times.

Attention, everyone!

BLESSED are You, God our God, King of the universe, who creates the fruit of the vine.

Distribute a bit to each of those assembled, and drink at least one and half ounces (45 ml) of the remaining wine while seated.

Passover Kiddush for Daytime on Shabbat

When a festival or Chol Hamoed occurs on Shabbat, the following sections are said quietly.

מִזְמוֹר לְדָוִד, יְיָ רֹעִי לֹא אֶחְסָר: בִּנְאוֹת דֶּשֶׁא יַרְבִּיצֵנִי, עַל מֵי מְנֻחוֹת יְנַהֲלֵנִי: נַפְשִׁי יְשׁוֹבֵב, יַנְחֵנִי בְמַעְגְּלֵי צֶדֶק לְמַעַן שְׁמוֹ: גַּם כִּי אֵלֵךְ בְּגֵיא צַלְמָוֶת לֹא אִירָא רָע, כִּי אַתָּה עִמָּדִי, שִׁבְטְךָ וּמִשְׁעַנְתֶּךָ הֵמָּה יְנַחֲמֻנִי: תַּעֲרֹךְ לְפָנַי שֻׁלְחָן נֶגֶד צֹרְרָי, דִּשַּׁנְתָּ בַשֶּׁמֶן רֹאשִׁי, כּוֹסִי רְוָיָה: אַךְ טוֹב וָחֶסֶד יִרְדְּפוּנִי כָּל יְמֵי חַיָּי, וְשַׁבְתִּי בְּבֵית יְיָ לְאֹרֶךְ יָמִים:

A Psalm by David. God is my shepherd; I shall lack nothing. He makes me lie down in green pastures; He leads me beside still waters. He revives my soul; He directs me in paths of righteousness for the sake of His Name. Even if I will walk in the valley of the shadow of death, I will fear no evil, for You are with me; Your rod and Your staff—they will comfort me. You will prepare a table for me before my enemies; You have anointed my head with oil; my cup is full. Only goodness and kindness shall follow me all the days of my life, and I shall dwell in the House of God for many long years.

אַתְקִינוּ סְעוּדָתָא דִמְהֵימְנוּתָא שְׁלֵמָתָא חֶדְוָתָא דְמַלְכָּא קַדִּישָׁא: אַתְקִינוּ סְעוּדָתָא דְמַלְכָּא, דָּא הִיא סְעוּדָתָא דְעַתִּיקָא קַדִּישָׁא, וַחֲקַל תַּפּוּחִין קַדִּישִׁין וּזְעֵיר אַנְפִּין אָתְיָן לְסַעֲדָא בַּהֲדֵיהּ:

PREPARE the meal of perfect faith, which is the delight of the holy King; prepare the meal of the King. This is the meal of the holy Ancient One, and the holy *Chakal Tapuchin* and *Z'eir Anpin* come to join Him in the meal.

וְשָׁמְרוּ בְנֵי יִשְׂרָאֵל אֶת הַשַּׁבָּת, לַעֲשׂוֹת אֶת הַשַּׁבָּת לְדֹרֹתָם בְּרִית עוֹלָם. בֵּינִי וּבֵין בְּנֵי יִשְׂרָאֵל אוֹת הִיא לְעֹלָם, כִּי שֵׁשֶׁת יָמִים עָשָׂה יְיָ אֶת הַשָּׁמַיִם וְאֶת הָאָרֶץ, וּבַיּוֹם הַשְּׁבִיעִי שָׁבַת וַיִּנָּפַשׁ:

AND the Children of Israel shall observe the Shabbat, establishing the Shabbat throughout their generations as an everlasting covenant. It is a sign between Me and the children of Israel for all time, for in six days God made the heavens and the earth, and on the seventh day He ceased from work and rested.

אַתְקִינוּ סְעוּדָתָא דִמְהֵימְנוּתָא שְׁלֵמָתָא חֶדְוָתָא דְמַלְכָּא קַדִּישָׁא. אַתְקִינוּ סְעוּדָתָא דְמַלְכָּא, דָּא הִיא סְעוּדָתָא דַּחֲקַל תַּפּוּחִין קַדִּישִׁין, וּזְעֵיר אַנְפִּין וְעַתִּיקָא קַדִּישָׁא אַתְיָן לְסַעֲדָא בַּהֲדַהּ:

PREPARE the meal of perfect faith, which is the delight of the holy King; prepare the meal of the King. This is the meal of the holy *Chakal Tapuchin,* and *Z'eir Anpin*[50] and the holy Ancient One[50] come to join her in the meal.[50]

Continue with Friday Night Kiddush for the Seder on page 26.

Passover Kiddush for Daytime

When a festival occurs on a weekday, recite the following before Kiddush.
(For daytime Kiddush for when Passover is on Shabbat, see the next page.)

אַתְקִינוּ סְעוּדָתָא דְמַלְכָּא שְׁלֵמָתָא חֶדְוָתָא דְמַלְכָּא קַדִּישָׁא, דָּא הִיא סְעוּדָתָא דְקוּדְשָׁא בְּרִיךְ הוּא וּשְׁכִינְתֵּהּ:

PREPARE the meal of the King, the complete delight of the holy King. This is the meal of the Holy One, blessed be He, and His Shechinah.

 Lift the cup and hold it in the palm of your right hand, and say:

אֵלֶּה מוֹעֲדֵי יְיָ, מִקְרָאֵי קֹדֶשׁ, אֲשֶׁר תִּקְרְאוּ אֹתָם בְּמוֹעֲדָם:

THESE are the festivals of God, holy assemblies, which you shall proclaim at their appointed times.

סַבְרִי מָרָנָן:

Attention, everyone!

בָּרוּךְ אַתָּה יְיָ, אֱלֹהֵינוּ מֶלֶךְ הָעוֹלָם, בּוֹרֵא פְּרִי הַגָּפֶן:

BLESSED are You, God our God, King of the universe, who creates the fruit of the vine.

Distribute a bit to each of those assembled, and drink at least one and half ounces (45 ml) of the remaining wine while seated.

סָדִין עָשְׂתָה וַתִּמְכֹּר, וַחֲגוֹר נָתְנָה לַכְּנַעֲנִי.	She makes a cloak and sells it, and she gives a belt to the merchant.
עֹז וְהָדָר לְבוּשָׁהּ, וַתִּשְׂחַק לְיוֹם אַחֲרוֹן.	She is robed in strength and dignity, and cheerfully faces whatever may come.
פִּיהָ פָּתְחָה בְחָכְמָה, וְתוֹרַת חֶסֶד עַל לְשׁוֹנָהּ.	She opens her mouth with wisdom; her tongue teaches loving-kindness.
צוֹפִיָּה הֲלִיכוֹת בֵּיתָהּ, וְלֶחֶם עַצְלוּת לֹא תֹאכֵל.	She tends to the affairs of her household, and does not eat the bread of idleness.
קָמוּ בָנֶיהָ וַיְאַשְּׁרוּהָ, בַּעְלָהּ וַיְהַלְלָהּ.	Her children stand up and celebrate her; her husband too, and he praises her.
רַבּוֹת בָּנוֹת עָשׂוּ חָיִל, וְאַתְּ עָלִית עַל כֻּלָּנָה.	He says, "Many women have done superbly, but you surpass them all!"
שֶׁקֶר הַחֵן וְהֶבֶל הַיֹּפִי, אִשָּׁה יִרְאַת יְיָ הִיא תִתְהַלָּל.	Charm is deceitful, beauty is vain, but a God-fearing woman is to be praised.
תְּנוּ לָהּ מִפְּרִי יָדֶיהָ, וִיהַלְלוּהָ בַשְּׁעָרִים מַעֲשֶׂיהָ:	Place before her the fruit of her hands. Wherever people gather, her deeds will be her praise.[47]

מִזְמוֹר לְדָוִד, יְיָ רֹעִי לֹא אֶחְסָר. בִּנְאוֹת דֶּשֶׁא יַרְבִּיצֵנִי, עַל מֵי מְנֻחוֹת יְנַהֲלֵנִי. נַפְשִׁי יְשׁוֹבֵב, יַנְחֵנִי בְמַעְגְּלֵי צֶדֶק לְמַעַן שְׁמוֹ. גַּם כִּי אֵלֵךְ בְּגֵיא צַלְמָוֶת לֹא אִירָא רָע, כִּי אַתָּה עִמָּדִי, שִׁבְטְךָ וּמִשְׁעַנְתֶּךָ הֵמָּה יְנַחֲמֻנִי. תַּעֲרֹךְ לְפָנַי שֻׁלְחָן נֶגֶד צֹרְרָי, דִּשַּׁנְתָּ בַשֶּׁמֶן רֹאשִׁי, כּוֹסִי רְוָיָה. אַךְ טוֹב וָחֶסֶד יִרְדְּפוּנִי כָּל יְמֵי חַיָּי, וְשַׁבְתִּי בְּבֵית יְיָ לְאֹרֶךְ יָמִים:

A Psalm by David. God is my shepherd; I shall lack nothing. He makes me lie down in green pastures; He leads me beside still waters. He revives my soul; He directs me in paths of righteousness for the sake of His Name. Even if I will walk in the valley of the shadow of death, I will fear no evil, for You are with me; Your rod and Your staff—they will comfort me. You will prepare a table for me before my enemies; You have anointed my head with oil; my cup is full. Only goodness and kindness shall follow me all the days of my life, and I shall dwell in the House of God for many long years.[48]

דָּא הִיא סְעוּדָתָא דַחֲקַל תַּפּוּחִין קַדִּישִׁין:

THIS is the meal of the holy *Chakal Tapuchin*.[49]

A Woman of Valor

אֵשֶׁת חַיִל מִי יִמְצָא, וְרָחֹק מִפְּנִינִים מִכְרָהּ.

A woman of valor, who can find?

Her value cannot be compared to pearls.

בָּטַח בָּהּ לֵב בַּעְלָהּ, וְשָׁלָל לֹא יֶחְסָר.

Her husband trusts her, and she lacks nothing.

גְּמָלַתְהוּ טוֹב וְלֹא רָע, כֹּל יְמֵי חַיֶּיהָ.

She returns his goodness, but never his wrongs, all the days of her life.

דָּרְשָׁה צֶמֶר וּפִשְׁתִּים, וַתַּעַשׂ בְּחֵפֶץ כַּפֶּיהָ.

She seeks out wool and flax. She works on her own initiative with her hands.

הָיְתָה כָּאֳנִיּוֹת סוֹחֵר, מִמֶּרְחָק תָּבִיא לַחְמָהּ.

She is like the merchant ships, bringing her bread from afar.

וַתָּקָם בְּעוֹד לַיְלָה, וַתִּתֵּן טֶרֶף לְבֵיתָהּ, וְחֹק לְנַעֲרֹתֶיהָ.

She rises while it is still night and provides food for her household, sets tasks for her maids.

זָמְמָה שָׂדֶה וַתִּקָּחֵהוּ, מִפְּרִי כַפֶּיהָ נָטְעָה כָּרֶם.

She estimates the value of a field, and buys it. From her own earnings she plants a vineyard.

חָגְרָה בְעוֹז מָתְנֶיהָ, וַתְּאַמֵּץ זְרוֹעֹתֶיהָ.

She girds herself with strength and stretches out her arms courageously.

טָעֲמָה כִּי טוֹב סַחְרָהּ, לֹא יִכְבֶּה בַלַּיְלָה נֵרָהּ.

She reasons that her business is good. Her lamp does not go out at night.

יָדֶיהָ שִׁלְּחָה בַכִּישׁוֹר, וְכַפֶּיהָ תָּמְכוּ פָלֶךְ.

She stretches forth her hands onto the distaff, and her hands support the spindle.

כַּפָּהּ פָּרְשָׂה לֶעָנִי, וְיָדֶיהָ שִׁלְּחָה לָאֶבְיוֹן.

She opens her hand to the needy and extends her hand to the poor.

לֹא תִירָא לְבֵיתָהּ מִשָּׁלֶג, כִּי כָל בֵּיתָהּ לָבֻשׁ שָׁנִים.

Her household does not fear the cold, for they are all dressed in crimson.

מַרְבַדִּים עָשְׂתָה לָּהּ, שֵׁשׁ וְאַרְגָּמָן לְבוּשָׁהּ.

She makes beautiful bedspreads for herself; fine linen and purple wool are her clothes.

נוֹדָע בַּשְּׁעָרִים בַּעְלָהּ, בְּשִׁבְתּוֹ עִם זִקְנֵי אָרֶץ.

Her husband is known in the gates, sitting with the elders of the land.

Friday Night

SHALOM ALEICHEM & ESHET CHAYIL FOR FRIDAY EVENING

When the first night of Passover occurs on a Friday night, recite the following quietly.

Shalom Aleichem

All week long, tradition tells us, you are surrounded by angels. When it comes to Shabbat, however, two special angels arrive—the Shabbat angels. So we greet them. And then, before we eat, we wish them farewell.

שָׁלוֹם עֲלֵיכֶם מַלְאֲכֵי הַשָּׁרֵת מַלְאֲכֵי עֶלְיוֹן מִמֶּלֶךְ מַלְכֵי הַמְּלָכִים הַקָּדוֹשׁ בָּרוּךְ הוּא:

PEACE be unto you, ministering angels,
Angels from on high,
From the King of kings of kings,
The One Who is Holy, blessed be He.
Repeat three times

בּוֹאֲכֶם לְשָׁלוֹם מַלְאֲכֵי הַשָּׁלוֹם מַלְאֲכֵי עֶלְיוֹן מִמֶּלֶךְ מַלְכֵי הַמְּלָכִים הַקָּדוֹשׁ בָּרוּךְ הוּא:

ENTER in peace, angels of peace,
Angels from on high,
From the King of kings of kings,
The One Who is Holy, blessed be He.
Repeat three times

בָּרְכוּנִי לְשָׁלוֹם מַלְאֲכֵי הַשָּׁלוֹם מַלְאֲכֵי עֶלְיוֹן מִמֶּלֶךְ מַלְכֵי הַמְּלָכִים הַקָּדוֹשׁ בָּרוּךְ הוּא:

BLESS me with peace, angels of peace,
Angels from on high,
From the King of kings of kings,
The One Who is Holy, blessed be He.
Repeat three times

צֵאתְכֶם לְשָׁלוֹם מַלְאֲכֵי הַשָּׁלוֹם מַלְאֲכֵי עֶלְיוֹן מִמֶּלֶךְ מַלְכֵי הַמְּלָכִים הַקָּדוֹשׁ בָּרוּךְ הוּא:

LEAVE in peace, angels of peace,
Angels from on high,
From the King of kings of kings,
The One Who is Holy, blessed be He.
Repeat three times

כִּי מַלְאָכָיו יְצַוֶּה לָּךְ, לִשְׁמָרְךָ בְּכָל דְּרָכֶיךָ:

FOR He will instruct His angels on your behalf, to guard you in all your ways.

יְיָ יִשְׁמָר צֵאתְךָ וּבוֹאֶךָ, מֵעַתָּה וְעַד עוֹלָם:

God will guard your going and your coming now and for all time.

APPENDIX

Now everyone calls out:

לְשָׁנָה הַבָּאָה בִּירוּשָׁלָיִם:

NEXT YEAR IN JERUSALEM!

Leh-shah-nah hah-bah-ah bee-roo-shah-lah-yim!

IN SOME VERSIONS of the Haggadah, there is now a line in which we say that the Seder is now concluded, and ask God that next year we celebrate it over roasted lamb in Jerusalem. Our version of the Haggadah does not have it.

Why? Because a Jew can never really say that the Seder has ended. We never stop leaving Egypt, as every day is another exodus from the bondage of mundane existence, headed for the promised land—a world in which every human being is absolutely free in body and soul.

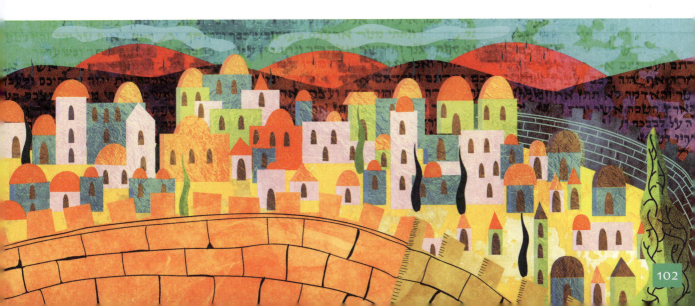

Drink the Fourth Cup

Raise your cup and say:

בָּרוּךְ אַתָּה יְיָ, אֱלֹהֵינוּ מֶלֶךְ הָעוֹלָם, בּוֹרֵא פְּרִי הַגָּפֶן:

BLESSED are You, God, our God, King of the universe, who creates the fruit of the vine.

Bah-rookh ah-tah ah-doh-noi eh-loh-hay-noo meh-lekh hah-oh-lahm boh-ray pree hah-gah-fehn.

Now lean to the left and drink your entire fourth cup of wine—or at least most of it.

Concluding Blessing for the Wine:

If you drank three ounces (86 ml) or more of wine:

בָּרוּךְ אַתָּה יְיָ, אֱלֹהֵינוּ מֶלֶךְ הָעוֹלָם, עַל הַגֶּפֶן וְעַל פְּרִי הַגֶּפֶן וְעַל תְּנוּבַת הַשָּׂדֶה וְעַל אֶרֶץ חֶמְדָּה טוֹבָה וּרְחָבָה שֶׁרָצִיתָ וְהִנְחַלְתָּ לַאֲבוֹתֵינוּ לֶאֱכוֹל מִפִּרְיָהּ וְלִשְׂבּוֹעַ מִטּוּבָהּ. רַחֵם נָא יְיָ אֱלֹהֵינוּ עַל יִשְׂרָאֵל עַמֶּךָ וְעַל יְרוּשָׁלַיִם עִירֶךָ וְעַל צִיּוֹן מִשְׁכַּן כְּבוֹדֶךָ וְעַל מִזְבְּחֶךָ וְעַל הֵיכָלֶךָ, וּבְנֵה יְרוּשָׁלַיִם עִיר הַקֹּדֶשׁ בִּמְהֵרָה בְיָמֵינוּ, וְהַעֲלֵנוּ לְתוֹכָהּ וְשַׂמְּחֵנוּ בָהּ וּנְבָרֶכְךָ בִּקְדֻשָּׁה וּבְטָהֳרָה.

BLESSED are You, God, our God, King of the universe, for the vine and the fruit of the vine,

for the produce of the field, and for the precious, good and spacious land which You have favored to give as a heritage to our fathers, to eat of its fruit and be satiated by its goodness.

Have mercy, God our God, on Israel Your people, on Jerusalem Your city, on Zion the abode of Your glory, on Your altar and on Your Temple.

Rebuild Jerusalem, the holy city, speedily in our days, and bring us up into it, and make us rejoice in it, and we will bless You in holiness and purity.

On Shabbat, add:

(וּרְצֵה וְהַחֲלִיצֵנוּ בְּיוֹם הַשַּׁבָּת הַזֶּה.)

(and may it please You to strengthen us on this Shabbat day.)

וְזָכְרֵנוּ לְטוֹבָה בְּיוֹם חַג הַמַּצּוֹת הַזֶּה. כִּי אַתָּה יְיָ טוֹב וּמֵטִיב לַכֹּל וְנוֹדֶה לְךָ עַל הָאָרֶץ וְעַל פְּרִי הַגָּפֶן. בָּרוּךְ אַתָּה יְיָ, עַל הָאָרֶץ וְעַל פְּרִי הַגָּפֶן:

And remember us for good on this day of the Festival of Matzot. For You, God, are good and do good to all, and we thank You for the land and for the fruit of the vine. Blessed are You, God, for the land and for the fruit of the vine.

Final Blessing on the Hallel

AND therefore may Your Name be praised forever, our King, the great and holy God and King in heaven and on earth. For to You, God our God and God of our fathers, it is always so pleasing to give song and praise, laud and hymn, strength and dominion, victory, greatness and might, glory, splendor, holiness and sovereignty; blessings and thanksgivings to Your great and holy Name. From the beginning to the end of the world You are Almighty God. Blessed are You, God, Almighty God, King, great and extolled in praises, God of thanksgivings, Lord of wonders, Creator of all souls, Master of all creatures, who takes pleasure in songs of praise; the only king, the Life of all worlds.

וּבְכֵן יִשְׁתַּבַּח שִׁמְךָ לָעַד מַלְכֵּנוּ, הָאֵל, הַמֶּלֶךְ הַגָּדוֹל וְהַקָּדוֹשׁ בַּשָּׁמַיִם וּבָאָרֶץ. כִּי לְךָ נָאֶה יְיָ אֱלֹהֵינוּ וֵאלֹהֵי אֲבוֹתֵינוּ לְעוֹלָם וָעֶד: שִׁיר וּשְׁבָחָה, הַלֵּל וְזִמְרָה, עֹז וּמֶמְשָׁלָה, נֶצַח, גְּדֻלָּה וּגְבוּרָה, תְּהִלָּה וְתִפְאֶרֶת, קְדֻשָּׁה וּמַלְכוּת: בְּרָכוֹת וְהוֹדָאוֹת לְשִׁמְךָ הַגָּדוֹל וְהַקָּדוֹשׁ, וּמֵעוֹלָם עַד עוֹלָם אַתָּה אֵל. בָּרוּךְ אַתָּה יְיָ, אֵל מֶלֶךְ גָּדוֹל וּמְהֻלָּל בַּתִּשְׁבָּחוֹת, אֵל הַהוֹדָאוֹת, אֲדוֹן הַנִּפְלָאוֹת, בּוֹרֵא כָּל הַנְּשָׁמוֹת, רִבּוֹן כָּל הַמַּעֲשִׂים, הַבּוֹחֵר בְּשִׁירֵי זִמְרָה, מֶלֶךְ יָחִיד חֵי הָעוֹלָמִים:

מִי יִדְמֶה לָּךְ, וּמִי יִשְׁוֶה לָּךְ, וּמִי יַעֲרָךְ לָךְ, הָאֵל הַגָּדוֹל, הַגִּבּוֹר וְהַנּוֹרָא, אֵל עֶלְיוֹן, קֹנֵה שָׁמַיִם וָאָרֶץ. נְהַלֶּלְךָ, וּנְשַׁבֵּחֲךָ, וּנְפָאֶרְךָ, וּנְבָרֵךְ אֶת שֵׁם קָדְשֶׁךָ, כָּאָמוּר: לְדָוִד, בָּרְכִי נַפְשִׁי אֶת יְיָ, וְכָל קְרָבַי אֶת שֵׁם קָדְשׁוֹ:

Who can be likened to You? Who is equal to You? Who can be compared to You?

The great, mighty, awesome God, God most high, owner of heaven and earth! We will laud You, praise You and glorify You, and we will bless Your holy Name, as it is said:

"A Psalm by David; Bless God, O my soul, and all that is within me bless His holy Name."

הָאֵל בְּתַעֲצֻמוֹת עֻזֶּךָ, הַגָּדוֹל בִּכְבוֹד שְׁמֶךָ, הַגִּבּוֹר לָנֶצַח, וְהַנּוֹרָא בְּנוֹרְאוֹתֶיךָ, הַמֶּלֶךְ הַיּוֹשֵׁב עַל כִּסֵּא רָם וְנִשָּׂא: שׁוֹכֵן עַד, מָרוֹם וְקָדוֹשׁ שְׁמוֹ, וְכָתוּב: רַנְּנוּ צַדִּיקִים בַּייָ, לַיְשָׁרִים נָאוָה תְהִלָּה: בְּפִי יְשָׁרִים תִּתְרוֹמָם, וּבְשִׂפְתֵי צַדִּיקִים תִּתְבָּרַךְ, וּבִלְשׁוֹן חֲסִידִים תִּתְקַדָּשׁ, וּבְקֶרֶב קְדוֹשִׁים תִּתְהַלָּל:

You are the Almighty God in the intensity of Your strength; Great in the glory of Your Name;

the Mighty forever, and the Awesome in Your awesome deeds; the king who sits upon a lofty and exalted throne. He who dwells for eternity, lofty and holy is His Name.

And it is written: "Sing joyously to God, you righteous; it is beautiful for the upright to offer praise." By the mouth of the upright You are exalted; by the lips of the righteous You are blessed; by the tongue of the pious You are sanctified; and among the holy ones You are praised.

וּבְמַקְהֲלוֹת רִבְבוֹת עַמְּךָ בֵּית יִשְׂרָאֵל, בְּרִנָּה יִתְפָּאֵר שִׁמְךָ מַלְכֵּנוּ בְּכָל דּוֹר וָדוֹר. שֶׁכֵּן חוֹבַת כָּל הַיְצוּרִים, לְפָנֶיךָ יְיָ אֱלֹהֵינוּ וֵאלֹהֵי אֲבוֹתֵינוּ: לְהוֹדוֹת, לְהַלֵּל, לְשַׁבֵּחַ, לְפָאֵר, לְרוֹמֵם, לְהַדֵּר, לְבָרֵךְ, לְעַלֵּה וּלְקַלֵּס, עַל כָּל דִּבְרֵי שִׁירוֹת וְתִשְׁבְּחוֹת דָּוִד בֶּן יִשַׁי עַבְדְּךָ מְשִׁיחֶךָ:

In assemblies of the myriads of Your people, the House of Israel, Your Name, our king, shall be glorified with song in every generation. For such is the obligation of all creatures before You, God our God and God of our fathers, to thank, to laud, to praise, to glorify, to exalt, to adore, to bless, to elevate and to honor You, even beyond all the words of songs and praises of David, son of Yishai, Your anointed servant.

If our hands would be spread out like the eagles of heaven, and our feet swift like deer, we would still be unable to thank You, God our God and God of our fathers, and to bless Your Name,

for even one of the thousands of millions, and myriads of myriads, of favors, miracles and wonders which You have done for us and for our fathers before us.

You have liberated us from Egypt, God our God.

You have freed us from the house of slavery,

You have fed us in famine and nourished us in plenty;

You have saved us from the sword and delivered us from illness, and raised us from evil and lasting diseases.

Until now Your mercies have helped us, and Your kindnesses have not forsaken us; and do not abandon us, God our God, forever!

וְיָדֵינוּ פְרוּשׂוֹת כְּנִשְׁרֵי שָׁמַיִם, וְרַגְלֵינוּ קַלּוֹת כָּאַיָּלוֹת, אֵין אֲנוּ מַסְפִּיקִים לְהוֹדוֹת לְךָ יְיָ אֱלֹהֵינוּ וֵאלֹהֵי אֲבוֹתֵינוּ, וּלְבָרֵךְ אֶת שְׁמֶךָ עַל אַחַת מֵאֶלֶף אַלְפֵי אֲלָפִים, וְרִבֵּי רְבָבוֹת פְּעָמִים, הַטּוֹבוֹת נִסִּים וְנִפְלָאוֹת שֶׁעָשִׂיתָ עִמָּנוּ וְעִם אֲבוֹתֵינוּ מִלְּפָנִים: מִמִּצְרַיִם גְּאַלְתָּנוּ, יְיָ אֱלֹהֵינוּ, מִבֵּית עֲבָדִים פְּדִיתָנוּ, בְּרָעָב זַנְתָּנוּ, וּבְשָׂבָע כִּלְכַּלְתָּנוּ, מֵחֶרֶב הִצַּלְתָּנוּ, וּמִדֶּבֶר מִלַּטְתָּנוּ, וּמֵחֳלָיִם רָעִים וְנֶאֱמָנִים דִּלִּיתָנוּ. עַד הֵנָּה עֲזָרוּנוּ רַחֲמֶיךָ, וְלֹא עֲזָבוּנוּ חֲסָדֶיךָ, וְאַל תִּטְּשֵׁנוּ יְיָ אֱלֹהֵינוּ, לָנֶצַח.

Therefore, the limbs which You have arranged within us, and the spirit and soul which You have breathed into our nostrils,

and the tongue which You have placed in our mouth—they all shall thank, bless, praise, glorify, exalt, adore, sanctify and proclaim the sovereignty of Your Name, our king.

For every mouth shall offer thanks to You,

every tongue shall swear by You, every eye shall look to You, every knee shall bend to You,

all who stand erect shall bow down before You, all hearts shall fear You, and every innermost part shall sing praise to Your Name,

as it is written:

"All my bones will say, God, who is like You;

You save the poor from one stronger than he,

the poor and the needy from one who would rob him!"

עַל כֵּן, אֵבָרִים שֶׁפִּלַּגְתָּ בָּנוּ, וְרוּחַ וּנְשָׁמָה שֶׁנָּפַחְתָּ בְּאַפֵּינוּ, וְלָשׁוֹן אֲשֶׁר שַׂמְתָּ בְּפִינוּ. הֵן הֵם: יוֹדוּ וִיבָרְכוּ וִישַׁבְּחוּ וִיפָאֲרוּ, וִירוֹמְמוּ וְיַעֲרִיצוּ, וְיַקְדִּישׁוּ וְיַמְלִיכוּ אֶת שִׁמְךָ מַלְכֵּנוּ. כִּי כָל פֶּה לְךָ יוֹדֶה, וְכָל לָשׁוֹן לְךָ תִשָּׁבַע, וְכָל עַיִן לְךָ תְצַפֶּה, וְכָל בֶּרֶךְ לְךָ תִכְרַע, וְכָל קוֹמָה לְפָנֶיךָ תִשְׁתַּחֲוֶה, וְכָל הַלְּבָבוֹת יִירָאוּךָ, וְכָל קֶרֶב וּכְלָיוֹת יְזַמְּרוּ לִשְׁמֶךָ, כַּדָּבָר שֶׁכָּתוּב: כָּל עַצְמוֹתַי תֹּאמַרְנָה, יְיָ, מִי כָמוֹךָ, מַצִּיל עָנִי מֵחָזָק מִמֶּנּוּ, וְעָנִי וְאֶבְיוֹן מִגֹּזְלוֹ:

Every Breath

נִשְׁמַת כָּל חַי תְּבָרֵךְ אֶת שִׁמְךָ יְיָ אֱלֹהֵינוּ, וְרוּחַ כָּל בָּשָׂר תְּפָאֵר וּתְרוֹמֵם זִכְרְךָ מַלְכֵּנוּ תָּמִיד, מִן הָעוֹלָם וְעַד הָעוֹלָם אַתָּה אֵל, וּמִבַּלְעָדֶיךָ אֵין לָנוּ מֶלֶךְ גּוֹאֵל וּמוֹשִׁיעַ, פּוֹדֶה וּמַצִּיל וּמְפַרְנֵס וְעוֹנֶה וּמְרַחֵם בְּכָל עֵת צָרָה וְצוּקָה, אֵין לָנוּ מֶלֶךְ אֶלָּא אַתָּה, אֱלֹהֵי הָרִאשׁוֹנִים וְהָאַחֲרוֹנִים. אֱלוֹהַּ כָּל בְּרִיּוֹת, אֲדוֹן כָּל תּוֹלָדוֹת, הַמְהֻלָּל בְּרֹב הַתִּשְׁבָּחוֹת, הַמְנַהֵג עוֹלָמוֹ בְּחֶסֶד וּבְרִיּוֹתָיו בְּרַחֲמִים.

THE breath of every living being shall bless Your Name, God our God;

and the spirit of all flesh shall always glorify and exalt the mention of You, our King.

From the beginning to the end of the world, You are Almighty God; and other than You we have no king, liberator and rescuer who delivers, saves, sustains, answers and is merciful in every time of trouble and distress.

We have no king but You.

You are God of the first and the last generations,

God of all creatures, Lord of all events, who is extolled with multiple praises, who directs His world with loving-kindness and His creatures with compassion.

וַיְיָ הִנֵּה לֹא יָנוּם וְלֹא יִישָׁן, הַמְעוֹרֵר יְשֵׁנִים, וְהַמֵּקִיץ נִרְדָּמִים, וְהַמֵּשִׂיחַ אִלְּמִים, וְהַמַּתִּיר אֲסוּרִים, וְהַסּוֹמֵךְ נוֹפְלִים, וְהַזּוֹקֵף כְּפוּפִים,

Behold, God neither slumbers nor sleeps. He arouses those who sleep and awakens those who slumber, enables the mute to speak, releases the bound, supports the falling and raises up those who are bowed.

לְךָ לְבַדְּךָ אֲנַחְנוּ מוֹדִים.

אִלּוּ פִינוּ מָלֵא שִׁירָה כַּיָּם, וּלְשׁוֹנֵנוּ רִנָּה כַּהֲמוֹן גַּלָּיו, וְשִׂפְתוֹתֵינוּ שֶׁבַח כְּמֶרְחֲבֵי רָקִיעַ, וְעֵינֵינוּ מְאִירוֹת כַּשֶּׁמֶשׁ וְכַיָּרֵחַ,

To You alone we give thanks.

Even if our mouths were filled with song as the sea, and our tongues with joyous singing like the multitudes of its waves;

If our lips would be filled with praise like the expanse of the sky, and our eyes shining like the sun and the moon;

וְנִעֵר פַּרְעֹה וְחֵילוֹ בְיַם סוּף, (ה) כִּי לְעוֹלָם חַסְדּוֹ:	And cast Pharaoh and his army into the Sea of Reeds—because His loving-kindness is infinite!
לְמוֹלִיךְ עַמּוֹ בַּמִּדְבָּר, כִּי לְעוֹלָם חַסְדּוֹ:	Who led His people through the desert— because His loving-kindness is infinite!
לְמַכֵּה מְלָכִים גְּדֹלִים, כִּי לְעוֹלָם חַסְדּוֹ:	Who struck great kings— because His loving-kindness is infinite!
וַיַּהֲרֹג מְלָכִים אַדִּירִים, כִּי לְעוֹלָם חַסְדּוֹ:	And slew super-powerful kings— because His loving-kindness is infinite!
לְסִיחוֹן מֶלֶךְ הָאֱמֹרִי, כִּי לְעוֹלָם חַסְדּוֹ:	Sichon, king of the Amorites— because His loving-kindness is infinite!
וּלְעוֹג מֶלֶךְ הַבָּשָׁן, כִּי לְעוֹלָם חַסְדּוֹ:	And Og, king of Bashan— because His loving-kindness is infinite!
וְנָתַן אַרְצָם לְנַחֲלָה, (ו) כִּי לְעוֹלָם חַסְדּוֹ:	And gave their land as a heritage— because His loving-kindness is infinite!
נַחֲלָה לְיִשְׂרָאֵל עַבְדּוֹ, כִּי לְעוֹלָם חַסְדּוֹ:	A heritage to Israel, His servant— because His loving-kindness is infinite!
שֶׁבְּשִׁפְלֵנוּ זָכַר לָנוּ, כִּי לְעוֹלָם חַסְדּוֹ:	Who remembered us when we were down— because His loving-kindness is infinite!
וַיִּפְרְקֵנוּ מִצָּרֵינוּ, כִּי לְעוֹלָם חַסְדּוֹ:	And delivered us from our oppressors— because His loving-kindness is infinite!
נוֹתֵן לֶחֶם לְכָל בָּשָׂר, כִּי לְעוֹלָם חַסְדּוֹ:	Who gives food to all living creatures— because His loving-kindness is infinite!
הוֹדוּ לְאֵל הַשָּׁמָיִם, (ה) כִּי לְעוֹלָם חַסְדּוֹ:	Thank God of heaven— because His loving-kindness is infinite!

הוֹדוּ לַיְיָ כִּי טוֹב, כִּי לְעוֹלָם חַסְדּוֹ:

הוֹדוּ לֵאלֹהֵי הָאֱלֹהִים,
כִּי לְעוֹלָם חַסְדּוֹ:

הוֹדוּ לַאֲדֹנֵי הָאֲדֹנִים,
כִּי לְעוֹלָם חַסְדּוֹ:

לְעֹשֵׂה נִפְלָאוֹת גְּדֹלוֹת לְבַדּוֹ,
כִּי לְעוֹלָם חַסְדּוֹ:

לְעֹשֵׂה הַשָּׁמַיִם בִּתְבוּנָה,
כִּי לְעוֹלָם חַסְדּוֹ:

לְרוֹקַע הָאָרֶץ עַל הַמָּיִם,
כִּי לְעוֹלָם חַסְדּוֹ:

לְעֹשֵׂה אוֹרִים גְּדֹלִים,
כִּי לְעוֹלָם חַסְדּוֹ:

אֶת הַשֶּׁמֶשׁ לְמֶמְשֶׁלֶת בַּיּוֹם,
כִּי לְעוֹלָם חַסְדּוֹ:

אֶת הַיָּרֵחַ וְכוֹכָבִים לְמֶמְשְׁלוֹת בַּלָּיְלָה,
כִּי לְעוֹלָם חַסְדּוֹ:

לְמַכֵּה מִצְרַיִם בִּבְכוֹרֵיהֶם,
כִּי לְעוֹלָם חַסְדּוֹ:

וַיּוֹצֵא יִשְׂרָאֵל מִתּוֹכָם,
כִּי לְעוֹלָם חַסְדּוֹ:

בְּיָד חֲזָקָה וּבִזְרוֹעַ נְטוּיָה,
כִּי לְעוֹלָם חַסְדּוֹ:

לְגֹזֵר יַם סוּף לִגְזָרִים,
כִּי לְעוֹלָם חַסְדּוֹ:

וְהֶעֱבִיר יִשְׂרָאֵל בְּתוֹכוֹ,
כִּי לְעוֹלָם חַסְדּוֹ:

THANK God, everyone, because He is good—
because His loving-kindness is infinite!

Thank the Almighty God of the mighty angels—
because His loving-kindness is infinite!

Thank the Master of the celestial hosts—
because His loving-kindness is infinite!

Who alone does great wonders—
because His loving-kindness is infinite!

Who made the heavens with intelligence—
because His loving-kindness is infinite!

Who stretched out the earth above the waters—
because His loving-kindness is infinite!

Who made the great lights—
because His loving-kindness is infinite!

The sun, to rule by day—
because His loving-kindness is infinite!

The moon and stars, to rule by night—
because His loving-kindness is infinite!

Who struck Egypt through their firstborn—
because His loving-kindness is infinite!

And brought Israel out of their midst—
because His loving-kindness is infinite!

With a strong hand and with an outstretched arm—because His loving-kindness is infinite!

Who split the Sea of Reeds into multiple avenues—because His loving-kindness is infinite!

And led Israel through it—
because His loving-kindness is infinite!

יְהַלְלוּךָ יְיָ אֱלֹהֵינוּ (עַל) כָּל מַעֲשֶׂיךָ, וַחֲסִידֶיךָ צַדִּיקִים עוֹשֵׂי רְצוֹנֶךָ, וְכָל עַמְּךָ בֵּית יִשְׂרָאֵל, בְּרִנָּה יוֹדוּ וִיבָרְכוּ, וִישַׁבְּחוּ וִיפָאֲרוּ, וִירוֹמְמוּ וְיַעֲרִיצוּ, וְיַקְדִּישׁוּ וְיַמְלִיכוּ אֶת שִׁמְךָ מַלְכֵּנוּ. כִּי לְךָ טוֹב לְהוֹדוֹת, וּלְשִׁמְךָ נָאֶה לְזַמֵּר, כִּי מֵעוֹלָם וְעַד עוֹלָם אַתָּה אֵל:

GOD our God, all Your works shall praise You;

Your pious ones, the righteous who do Your will,

and all Your people, the House of Israel,

with joyous song will thank and bless,

laud and glorify, exalt and adore,

sanctify and proclaim the sovereignty of Your Name, our King.

For it is good to thank You,

and befitting to sing to Your Name,

for from the beginning to the end of the world

You are Almighty God.

Up to this point, we've read what's called "The Egyptian Hallel." Now comes chapter 136 of Psalms, which is called "The Great Hallel." This has 26 verses lauding God's infinite kindness, corresponding to the 26 generations of humankind that survived free of charge before the Torah was given. Once the Torah was given, there was a whole new dimension of accountability to life. That's an even greater kindness. So, really, life is all about God's infinite loving-kindness.

Twenty-six is also the sum you get when adding up the numerical value of the letters of God's name. (In Hebrew, every letter has a numerical value.)

Pronounced:

Ah-nah ah-doh-noi hoh-shee-ah nah!
Ah-nah ah-doh-noi hoh-shee-ah nah!
Ah-nah ah-doh-noi hahtz-lee-khah nah!
Ah-nah ah-doh-noi hahtz-lee-khah nah!

בָּרוּךְ הַבָּא בְּשֵׁם יְיָ, בֵּרַכְנוּכֶם מִבֵּית יְיָ: בָּרוּךְ הַבָּא בְּשֵׁם יְיָ, בֵּרַכְנוּכֶם מִבֵּית יְיָ: אֵל יְיָ וַיָּאֶר לָנוּ, אִסְרוּ חַג בַּעֲבֹתִים, עַד קַרְנוֹת הַמִּזְבֵּחַ: אֵל יְיָ וַיָּאֶר לָנוּ, אִסְרוּ חַג בַּעֲבֹתִים, עַד קַרְנוֹת הַמִּזְבֵּחַ:

BLESSED is he who comes in the Name of God;

we bless you from the House of God.

Blessed is he who comes in the Name of God;

we bless you from the House of God.

God is Almighty and He shines to us; therefore you should tie up your festival-offering until you get it to the altar.

God is Almighty, He gave us light; bind the festival-offering until you bring it to the horns of the altar.

אֵלִי אַתָּה וְאוֹדֶךָּ, אֱלֹהַי אֲרוֹמְמֶךָּ:
אֵלִי אַתָּה וְאוֹדֶךָּ, אֱלֹהַי אֲרוֹמְמֶךָּ:

You are my God and I will thank You; my God, I will exalt You.

You are my God and I will thank You; my God, I will exalt You.

הוֹדוּ לַייָ כִּי טוֹב, כִּי לְעוֹלָם חַסְדּוֹ:
הוֹדוּ לַייָ כִּי טוֹב, כִּי לְעוֹלָם חַסְדּוֹ:

Thank God, everybody, for He is good, for His loving-kindness is infinite.

Thank God, everybody, for He is good, for His loving-kindness is infinite.

פִּתְחוּ לִי שַׁעֲרֵי צֶדֶק, אָבֹא בָם אוֹדֶה יָהּ: זֶה הַשַּׁעַר לַיְיָ, צַדִּיקִים יָבֹאוּ בוֹ:	Open for me the gates of righteousness; I will enter them and give thanks to God. This is the gate of God; the righteous will enter through it.
אוֹדְךָ כִּי עֲנִיתָנִי, וַתְּהִי לִי לִישׁוּעָה: אוֹדְךָ כִּי עֲנִיתָנִי, וַתְּהִי לִי לִישׁוּעָה:	I thank You for You have answered me, and You have been a help to me. I thank You for You have answered me, and You have been a help to me.
אֶבֶן מָאֲסוּ הַבּוֹנִים, הָיְתָה לְרֹאשׁ פִּנָּה: אֶבֶן מָאֲסוּ הַבּוֹנִים, הָיְתָה לְרֹאשׁ פִּנָּה:	We were the stone scorned by the builders, but we became the main cornerstone of this world. We were the stone scorned by the builders, but we became the main cornerstone of this world.
מֵאֵת יְיָ הָיְתָה זֹּאת, הִיא נִפְלָאת בְּעֵינֵינוּ: מֵאֵת יְיָ הָיְתָה זֹּאת, הִיא נִפְלָאת בְּעֵינֵינוּ:	This was indeed from God; it is wondrous in our eyes. This was indeed from God; it is wondrous in our eyes.
זֶה הַיּוֹם עָשָׂה יְיָ, נָגִילָה וְנִשְׂמְחָה בוֹ: זֶה הַיּוֹם עָשָׂה יְיָ, נָגִילָה וְנִשְׂמְחָה בוֹ:	This is a day that God has made special; let's rejoice and celebrate on it. This is a day that God has made special; let's rejoice and celebrate on it.

 THE SAGES of the Talmud teach that the ultimate exodus for which we all yearn could come in one of two ways: If we merit, it could be jump-started early. But if we don't, it will just happen in its time no matter what.

Here we ask God to take the first option.[46]

The leader reads each of these four lines out loud, and everyone repeats, line by line:

אָנָּא יְיָ הוֹשִׁיעָה נָּא:	O God, please help us right now!
אָנָּא יְיָ הוֹשִׁיעָה נָּא:	O God, please help us right now!
אָנָּא יְיָ הַצְלִיחָה נָּא:	O God, please grant us success right now!
אָנָּא יְיָ הַצְלִיחָה נָּא:	O God, please grant us success right now!

מִן הַמֵּצַר קָרָאתִי יָּהּ, עָנָנִי בַמֶּרְחַב יָהּ: יְיָ לִי לֹא אִירָא, מַה יַּעֲשֶׂה לִי אָדָם: יְיָ לִי בְּעֹזְרָי, וַאֲנִי אֶרְאֶה בְשׂנְאָי: טוֹב לַחֲסוֹת בַּייָ, מִבְּטֹחַ בָּאָדָם: טוֹב לַחֲסוֹת בַּייָ, מִבְּטֹחַ בִּנְדִיבִים:

Out of a tight place, I called to God; God answered me with abounding relief.

God is with me, I will not fear—what can a human being do to me?

God is with me through my helpers, so I can face my enemies.

Better to rely on God than to trust in human beings.

Better to rely on God than to rely on philanthropists.

כָּל גּוֹיִם סְבָבוּנִי, בְּשֵׁם יְיָ כִּי אֲמִילַם: סַבּוּנִי גַם סְבָבוּנִי, בְּשֵׁם יְיָ כִּי אֲמִילַם: סַבּוּנִי כִדְבֹרִים דֹּעֲכוּ כְּאֵשׁ קוֹצִים, בְּשֵׁם יְיָ כִּי אֲמִילַם: דָּחֹה דְחִיתַנִי לִנְפֹּל, וַייָ עֲזָרָנִי: עָזִּי וְזִמְרָת יָהּ, וַיְהִי לִי לִישׁוּעָה:

All nations were at war all around me, but I trusted in God and cut through them.

They surrounded me, they encompassed me, but I cut through them by trusting God.

They surrounded me like bees, yet they were extinguished like thorns on fire; I cut through them by trusting in God.

They pushed me again and again to fall, but God helped me.

God is my strength and song, and He was there to rescue me.

קוֹל רִנָּה וִישׁוּעָה בְּאָהֳלֵי צַדִּיקִים, יְמִין יְיָ עֹשָׂה חָיִל: יְמִין יְיָ רוֹמֵמָה, יְמִין יְיָ עֹשָׂה חָיִל: לֹא אָמוּת כִּי אֶחְיֶה, וַאֲסַפֵּר מַעֲשֵׂי יָהּ: יַסֹּר יִסְּרַנִּי יָּהּ, וְלַמָּוֶת לֹא נְתָנָנִי:

There's a sound of joyous song of people who have been rescued coming from the tents of the righteous, singing:

"The right hand of God performs valiant deeds!

"The right hand of God is way up there! The right hand of God performs valiant deeds!"

I shall not die, but I shall live and tell the stories of God.

God chastised me, but He didn't let me die.

> If you have three or more people, one person leads and the others respond.
> Otherwise, just say the lines labeled "Others."

Leader: הוֹדוּ לַייָ כִּי טוֹב, כִּי לְעוֹלָם חַסְדּוֹ:
Give thanks to God, for He is good, because His loving-kindness is infinite!

Others: הוֹדוּ לַייָ כִּי טוֹב, כִּי לְעוֹלָם חַסְדּוֹ:
Give thanks to God, for He is good, because His loving-kindness is infinite!

יֹאמַר נָא יִשְׂרָאֵל, כִּי לְעוֹלָם חַסְדּוֹ:
Say it now, Israel, because His loving-kindness is infinite.

Leader: יֹאמַר נָא יִשְׂרָאֵל, כִּי לְעוֹלָם חַסְדּוֹ:
Say it now, Israel, because His loving-kindness is infinite.

Others: הוֹדוּ לַייָ כִּי טוֹב, כִּי לְעוֹלָם חַסְדּוֹ:
Give thanks to God, for He is good, because His loving-kindness is infinite.

יֹאמְרוּ נָא בֵית אַהֲרֹן, כִּי לְעוֹלָם חַסְדּוֹ:
Say it now, House of Aaron, because His loving-kindness is infinite.

Leader: יֹאמְרוּ נָא בֵית אַהֲרֹן, כִּי לְעוֹלָם חַסְדּוֹ:
Say it now, House of Aaron, because His loving-kindness is infinite.

Others: הוֹדוּ לַייָ כִּי טוֹב, כִּי לְעוֹלָם חַסְדּוֹ:
Give thanks to God, for He is good, because His loving-kindness is infinite.

יֹאמְרוּ נָא יִרְאֵי יְיָ, כִּי לְעוֹלָם חַסְדּוֹ:
Say it now, all people who are in awe of God, because His loving-kindness is infinite.

Leader: יֹאמְרוּ נָא יִרְאֵי יְיָ, כִּי לְעוֹלָם חַסְדּוֹ:
Say it now, all people who are in awe of God, because His loving-kindness is infinite.

Others: הוֹדוּ לַייָ כִּי טוֹב, כִּי לְעוֹלָם חַסְדּוֹ:
Give thanks to God, for He is good, because His loving-kindness is infinite.

Pronounced:

Leader: **Hoh-doo lah-doh-noi kee tohv kee leh-oh-lahm khahs-doh!**
Others: **Hoh-doo lah-doh-noi kee tohv kee leh-oh-lahm khahs-doh, Yoh-mahr nah yis-rah-ehl kee leh-oh-lahm khahs-doh!**
Leader: **Yoh-mahr nah yis-rah-ehl kee leh-oh-lahm khahs-doh!**
Others: **Hoh-doo lah-doh-noi kee tohv kee leh-oh-lahm khahs-doh. Yoh-meh-roo nah bayt ah-hah-rohn kee leh-oh-lahm khahs-doh!**
Leader: **Yoh-meh-roo nah bayt ah-hah-rohn kee leh-oh-lahm khahs-doh!**
Others: **Hoh-doo lah-doh-noi kee tohv kee leh-oh-lahm khahs-doh. Yoh-meh-roo nah yir-ay ah-doh-noi kee leh-oh-lahm khahs-doh!**
Leader: **yoh-meh-roo nah yir-ay ah-doh-noi kee leh-oh-lahm khahs-doh!**
Others: **Hoh-doo lah-doh-noi kee tohv kee leh-oh-lahm khahs-doh.**

THE TALMUD TELLS: There will come a day when Egypt will bring a gift for Moshiach. They'll figure he probably won't accept it from them. But the Holy One, may He be blessed, will say, "Accept it from them! They were hosts to My children in Egypt."

When the other nations see that the Egyptian offering was accepted, they will say, "For sure, ours will be as well!" And they'll all start bringing gifts, and praising their Creator as well.

Which teaches us that people do good things and bad things. For the bad things, they'll get their just deserts. For the good things, you should show your appreciation. It pays off.[45]

הַלְלוּ אֶת יְיָ כָּל גּוֹיִם,
שַׁבְּחוּהוּ כָּל הָאֻמִּים:
כִּי גָבַר עָלֵינוּ חַסְדּוֹ, וֶאֱמֶת יְיָ לְעוֹלָם,
הַלְלוּיָהּ:

CHEER God, all you nations!

Praise Him, all you peoples!

All the more so, we should thank Him, because His kindness went way over the top for us, and the truth of God is infinite.

Halleluyah!

אָהַבְתִּי, כִּי יִשְׁמַע יְיָ אֶת קוֹלִי תַּחֲנוּנָי: כִּי הִטָּה אָזְנוֹ לִי, וּבְיָמַי אֶקְרָא: אֲפָפוּנִי חֶבְלֵי מָוֶת, וּמְצָרֵי שְׁאוֹל מְצָאוּנִי, צָרָה וְיָגוֹן אֶמְצָא: וּבְשֵׁם יְיָ אֶקְרָא, אָנָּה יְיָ מַלְּטָה נַפְשִׁי: חַנּוּן יְיָ וְצַדִּיק, וֵאלֹהֵינוּ מְרַחֵם: שֹׁמֵר פְּתָאיִם יְיָ, דַּלֹּתִי וְלִי יְהוֹשִׁיעַ: שׁוּבִי נַפְשִׁי לִמְנוּחָיְכִי, כִּי יְיָ גָּמַל עָלָיְכִי: כִּי חִלַּצְתָּ נַפְשִׁי מִמָּוֶת, אֶת עֵינִי מִן דִּמְעָה, אֶת רַגְלִי מִדֶּחִי: אֶתְהַלֵּךְ לִפְנֵי יְיָ, בְּאַרְצוֹת הַחַיִּים: הֶאֱמַנְתִּי כִּי אֲדַבֵּר, אֲנִי עָנִיתִי מְאֹד: אֲנִי אָמַרְתִּי בְחָפְזִי, כָּל הָאָדָם כֹּזֵב:

I LOVE GOD, because He hears my voice, my prayers.

He pays attention to me any day I call. The pangs of death might encompass me, and the agonies of the grave catch up with me.

I could face trouble and sorrow, and I would call upon the Name of God, saying, "Please, God, get me out of this!"

God is gracious and just. Our God is compassionate. God watches over simple people (like me). I was really down, and He got me out of there. My soul, you can rest again, for God dealt kindly with you.

For You have delivered my soul from death, my eyes from tears, my foot from stumbling. I will walk before God in the lands of the living. Even when I said, "I am so down and out!"

—really, I still had faith. When I said, "All people are deceitful," I was just being too hasty.

מָה אָשִׁיב לַיְיָ, כָּל תַּגְמוּלוֹהִי עָלָי: כּוֹס יְשׁוּעוֹת אֶשָּׂא, וּבְשֵׁם יְיָ אֶקְרָא: נְדָרַי לַיְיָ אֲשַׁלֵּם, נֶגְדָה נָּא לְכָל עַמּוֹ: יָקָר בְּעֵינֵי יְיָ, הַמָּוְתָה לַחֲסִידָיו: אָנָּה יְיָ כִּי אֲנִי עַבְדֶּךָ, אֲנִי עַבְדְּךָ בֶּן אֲמָתֶךָ, פִּתַּחְתָּ לְמוֹסֵרָי: לְךָ אֶזְבַּח זֶבַח תּוֹדָה, וּבְשֵׁם יְיָ אֶקְרָא: נְדָרַי לַיְיָ אֲשַׁלֵּם, נֶגְדָה נָּא לְכָל עַמּוֹ: בְּחַצְרוֹת בֵּית יְיָ, בְּתוֹכֵכִי יְרוּשָׁלָיִם, הַלְלוּיָהּ:

WHAT can I repay God for all His kindness to me?

I will raise a cup to all the times You rescued me and call upon the name of God.

I will pay my vows to God in the presence of all His people.

God takes the death of His pious ones very seriously.

I thank you, God, for I am Your servant.

I am Your servant, the son of Your handmaid; You have loosened my bonds.

To You I will bring an offering of thanksgiving, and I will call upon the name of God.

I will pay my vows to God in the presence of all His people, in the courtyards of the House of God, in the midst of Jerusalem. *Halleluyah!* Praise God!

כְּמוֹהֶם יִהְיוּ עֹשֵׂיהֶם, כֹּל אֲשֶׁר בֹּטֵחַ בָּהֶם: יִשְׂרָאֵל בְּטַח בַּיְיָ, עֶזְרָם וּמָגִנָּם הוּא: בֵּית אַהֲרֹן בִּטְחוּ בַיְיָ, עֶזְרָם וּמָגִנָּם הוּא: יִרְאֵי יְיָ בִּטְחוּ בַיְיָ, עֶזְרָם וּמָגִנָּם הוּא: יְיָ זְכָרָנוּ יְבָרֵךְ, יְבָרֵךְ אֶת בֵּית יִשְׂרָאֵל, יְבָרֵךְ אֶת בֵּית אַהֲרֹן: יְבָרֵךְ יִרְאֵי יְיָ, הַקְּטַנִּים עִם הַגְּדֹלִים: יֹסֵף יְיָ עֲלֵיכֶם, עֲלֵיכֶם וְעַל בְּנֵיכֶם: בְּרוּכִים אַתֶּם לַיְיָ, עֹשֵׂה שָׁמַיִם וָאָרֶץ: הַשָּׁמַיִם שָׁמַיִם לַיְיָ, וְהָאָרֶץ נָתַן לִבְנֵי אָדָם: לֹא הַמֵּתִים יְהַלְלוּ יָהּ, וְלֹא כָּל יֹרְדֵי דוּמָה: וַאֲנַחְנוּ נְבָרֵךְ יָהּ, מֵעַתָּה וְעַד עוֹלָם, הַלְלוּיָהּ:

Those who produce them will end up like them, everyone that trusts in them.

But Israel, trust in God! He is their help and their shield.

House of Aaron, trust in God! He is their help and their shield.

All human beings who are in awe of God, trust in God! He is their help and their shield.

God, who is always mindful of us, will bless us.

He will bless the House of Israel; He will bless the House of Aaron;

He will bless all people who are in awe of God, the small ones along with the big ones.

May God give you more and more blessings, blessings for you and for your children!

You should be blessed over and over again by God, the Maker of heaven and earth.

The heavens are the heavens of God, but as for the earth, He assigned some responsibility to human beings.

The dead aren't going to cheer for God, all those that go down into the silence of the grave.

But we will bless God, from now to eternity. *Halleluyah!* Praise God!

"THOSE WHO ARE IN AWE OF GOD"—that's a reference to the righteous among the nations. According to Jewish tradition, you don't have to be Jewish to have a share in the World to Come. You just have to be righteous and keep the basic laws of humanity, as given to Adam and Noah by the Creator.

The times of Moshiach and the final exodus isn't just a liberation and homecoming for all the Jews. At that time, the entire world, every individual and every creature, will attain its fulfillment.

Like Maimonides writes, the entire occupation of the world will be just to know the divine wisdom. Everything that exists now will exist then, but our minds will be open to the awe and wonder of it all, and everyone will sing praises.

Hallel Nirtzah

Praise God for His Wonders!

The Hallel continues where we left off before the meal. It's a lot of fun if you know all the songs and sing them in Hebrew. If you don't know that, try to read it out loud in English. Make sure to say the last blessing, and drink the fourth and last cup of wine.

HALLEL IS A SECTION of the Psalms that were selected to be recited and sung together on those occasions when God really deserves some special recognition—as in when He has made miracles for us.

We already said Hallel in our prayers before the Seder on this night. But now we're saying it as part of the Seder.

We already said the first lines of Hallel just before we drank the second cup of wine. Those lines were about the Exodus from Egypt. Now we say the rest—which are about the upcoming liberation brought to us by Moshiach real soon.

We begin by explaining to God why He has to get this done real soon—because the current situation is real bad for His reputation. We continue by celebrating and praising Him for liberating us, because we're super-confident that He has accepted our plea and Moshiach is on his way.

לֹא לָנוּ יְיָ, לֹא לָנוּ, כִּי לְשִׁמְךָ תֵּן כָּבוֹד, עַל חַסְדְּךָ עַל אֲמִתֶּךָ: לָמָּה יֹאמְרוּ הַגּוֹיִם, אַיֵּה נָא אֱלֹהֵיהֶם: וֵאלֹהֵינוּ בַשָּׁמָיִם, כֹּל אֲשֶׁר חָפֵץ עָשָׂה: עֲצַבֵּיהֶם כֶּסֶף וְזָהָב, מַעֲשֵׂה יְדֵי אָדָם: פֶּה לָהֶם וְלֹא יְדַבֵּרוּ, עֵינַיִם לָהֶם וְלֹא יִרְאוּ: אָזְנַיִם לָהֶם וְלֹא יִשְׁמָעוּ, אַף לָהֶם וְלֹא יְרִיחוּן: יְדֵיהֶם וְלֹא יְמִישׁוּן, רַגְלֵיהֶם וְלֹא יְהַלֵּכוּ, לֹא יֶהְגּוּ בִּגְרוֹנָם:

DON'T do it for us, God! Not for us, but to give some honor to Your own name! For the sake of Your reputation for loving-kindness and being true to Your word!

Why should the nations say, "Where, now, is their God?"

Our God is in heaven; anything He desires, He makes it happen.

Their idols are of silver and gold, fabrications of human hands:

they have mouths, but cannot speak;

they have eyes, but cannot see;

they have ears, but cannot hear;

they have a nose, but cannot smell;

their hands cannot feel; their feet cannot walk;

no sound comes out of their throat.

Pour the Fourth Cup of Wine

Now it's time to pour the fourth cup, over which we will sing songs praising God for His wonders.

Pour the fourth cup, and if you haven't yet done so, pour a cup for Elijah the Prophet. Then we send someone to open all the doors leading from the dining table to the outside, so that Elijah can enter and announce that Moshiach is on his way. When it's not Friday night, many have the custom of taking along a lit candle from the table.

EVERYTHING WE DO on the night of the Seder is a reflection of what God Himself is up to on this night. We open all the doors from our place at the table until the outside door of our home because that is what is happening above.

For every prayer, heaven has many doors, each requiring another pass before it will open to you. Why do you deserve an answer to this prayer? What have you been doing with your life until now? When others asked for help, did you help them?

But on the two nights of Passover, all the doors are left wide open. Regardless of who you are, where you are standing, or even what you were doing a moment ago, tonight you can leap upwards to the highest heights.

Ask for whatever burns inside your heart to be asked. Think big. Think way up there. And yet higher.[44]

שְׁפֹךְ חֲמָתְךָ אֶל הַגּוֹיִם אֲשֶׁר לֹא יְדָעוּךָ, וְעַל מַמְלָכוֹת אֲשֶׁר בְּשִׁמְךָ לֹא קָרָאוּ: כִּי אָכַל אֶת יַעֲקֹב, וְאֶת נָוֵהוּ הֵשַׁמּוּ: שְׁפָךְ עֲלֵיהֶם זַעְמֶךָ וַחֲרוֹן אַפְּךָ יַשִּׂיגֵם: תִּרְדֹּף בְּאַף וְתַשְׁמִידֵם מִתַּחַת שְׁמֵי יְיָ:

POUR out Your wrath upon those nations that do not acknowledge You,

and upon the kingdoms that have never called upon Your Name.

For they have devoured Jacob and laid waste to his home.

Pour out Your wrath upon them, and let the wrath of Your anger overtake them.

Pursue them with anger, and destroy them from beneath the heavens of God.

To this day, there remain despots and masters of terror who connive every means they can to destroy us. These words are meant not only for them, but for all the forces of darkness and destruction, physical and spiritual, that plague us. Their elimination will be the greatest healing and liberation for this beautiful world that God has made.

You can now close whatever doors you opened. Wait for everyone to get back to the table before going on.

מִגְדַּל יְשׁוּעוֹת מַלְכּוֹ וְעֹשֶׂה חֶסֶד לִמְשִׁיחוֹ לְדָוִד וּלְזַרְעוֹ עַד עוֹלָם: עֹשֶׂה שָׁלוֹם בִּמְרוֹמָיו הוּא יַעֲשֶׂה שָׁלוֹם עָלֵינוּ וְעַל כָּל יִשְׂרָאֵל וְאִמְרוּ אָמֵן:

HE is a tower of salvation to His king, and bestows loving-kindness upon His anointed, to David and his descendants forever.

He who makes peace in His heights, may He make peace for us and for all Israel; and say, Amen.

יְראוּ אֶת יְיָ קְדֹשָׁיו, כִּי אֵין מַחְסוֹר לִירֵאָיו: כְּפִירִים רָשׁוּ וְרָעֵבוּ, וְדֹרְשֵׁי יְיָ לֹא יַחְסְרוּ כָל טוֹב: הוֹדוּ לַיְיָ כִּי טוֹב, כִּי לְעוֹלָם חַסְדּוֹ: פּוֹתֵחַ אֶת יָדֶךָ, וּמַשְׂבִּיעַ לְכָל חַי רָצוֹן: בָּרוּךְ הַגֶּבֶר אֲשֶׁר יִבְטַח בַּיְיָ, וְהָיָה יְיָ מִבְטַחוֹ:

BE in awe of God, you His holy ones, for those who are in awe of Him suffer no want. Young lions are in need and go hungry, but those who seek God shall not lack any good.

Give thanks to God, for He is good, because His loving-kindness is infinite.

You open Your hand and satisfy the desire of every living thing.

Blessed is the man who trusts in God, and God will be his trust.

Drink the Third Cup of Wine

 Hold the cup and say the blessing on the third cup of wine:

 Everyone:

בָּרוּךְ אַתָּה יְיָ, אֱלֹהֵינוּ מֶלֶךְ הָעוֹלָם, בּוֹרֵא פְּרִי הַגָּפֶן:

BLESSED are You, God our God, King of the universe, who creates the fruit of the vine.

Bah-rookh ah-tah ah-doh-noi eh-loh-hay-noo meh-lekh hah-oh-lahm boh-ray pree hah-gah-fehn.

Now lean to the left and drink your entire third cup of wine—or at least most of it.

הָרַחֲמָן הוּא יִשְׁלַח לָנוּ אֶת אֵלִיָּהוּ הַנָּבִיא זָכוּר לַטּוֹב וִיבַשֶּׂר לָנוּ בְּשׂוֹרוֹת טוֹבוֹת יְשׁוּעוֹת וְנֶחָמוֹת:

May the Compassionate One send us Elijah the Prophet, may he be remembered for good, and may he bring us good tidings, salvation and consolation.

הָרַחֲמָן הוּא יְבָרֵךְ אֶת אָבִי מוֹרִי בַּעַל הַבַּיִת הַזֶּה וְאֶת אִמִּי מוֹרָתִי בַּעֲלַת הַבַּיִת הַזֶּה אוֹתָם וְאֶת בֵּיתָם וְאֶת זַרְעָם וְאֶת כָּל אֲשֶׁר לָהֶם אוֹתָנוּ וְאֶת כָּל אֲשֶׁר לָנוּ: כְּמוֹ שֶׁבֵּרַךְ אֶת אֲבוֹתֵינוּ אַבְרָהָם יִצְחָק וְיַעֲקֹב בַּכֹּל מִכֹּל כֹּל, כֵּן יְבָרֵךְ אוֹתָנוּ (בְּנֵי בְרִית) כֻּלָּנוּ יַחַד בִּבְרָכָה שְׁלֵמָה וְנֹאמַר אָמֵן:

MAY the Compassionate One bless my father, my teacher, the master of this house, and my mother, my teacher, the mistress of this house; them, their household, their children, and all that is theirs; us, and all that is ours. Just as He blessed our forefathers, Abraham, Isaac and Jacob, "in everything," "from everything," "with everything," so may He bless all of us (the children of the Covenant) together with a perfect blessing, and let us say, Amen.

מִמָּרוֹם יְלַמְּדוּ עָלָיו וְעָלֵינוּ זְכוּת שֶׁתְּהֵא לְמִשְׁמֶרֶת שָׁלוֹם וְנִשָּׂא בְרָכָה מֵאֵת יְיָ וּצְדָקָה מֵאֱלֹהֵי יִשְׁעֵנוּ וְנִמְצָא חֵן וְשֵׂכֶל טוֹב בְּעֵינֵי אֱלֹהִים וְאָדָם:

FROM On High, may there be invoked upon him and upon us such merit as will bring a safeguarding of peace. May we receive blessing from God, and just loving-kindness from the God who rescues us, and may we find grace and good understanding in the eyes of God and man.

If it's Friday night, add the following in honor of Shabbat:

הָרַחֲמָן הוּא יַנְחִילֵנוּ לְיוֹם שֶׁכֻּלּוֹ שַׁבָּת וּמְנוּחָה לְחַיֵּי הָעוֹלָמִים:

MAY the Compassionate One give us our heritage of a day that is entirely Shabbat and rest for eternal life.

הָרַחֲמָן הוּא יַנְחִילֵנוּ לְיוֹם שֶׁכֻּלּוֹ טוֹב:

MAY the Compassionate One give us our heritage of a day which is all good.

הָרַחֲמָן הוּא יְזַכֵּנוּ לִימוֹת הַמָּשִׁיחַ וּלְחַיֵּי הָעוֹלָם הַבָּא.

MAY the Compassionate One privilege us with the days of Moshiach and the life of the World to Come.

Blessing Four

בָּרוּךְ אַתָּה יְיָ, אֱלֹהֵינוּ מֶלֶךְ הָעוֹלָם, הָאֵל, אָבִינוּ מַלְכֵּנוּ, אַדִירֵנוּ בּוֹרְאֵנוּ גּוֹאֲלֵנוּ יוֹצְרֵנוּ, קְדוֹשֵׁנוּ קְדוֹשׁ יַעֲקֹב, רוֹעֵנוּ רוֹעֵה יִשְׂרָאֵל הַמֶּלֶךְ הַטּוֹב וְהַמֵּטִיב לַכֹּל בְּכָל יוֹם וָיוֹם, הוּא הֵטִיב לָנוּ, הוּא מֵטִיב לָנוּ, הוּא יֵיטִיב לָנוּ, הוּא גְמָלָנוּ הוּא גוֹמְלֵנוּ הוּא יִגְמְלֵנוּ לָעַד, לְחֵן וּלְחֶסֶד וּלְרַחֲמִים, וּלְרֶוַח הַצָּלָה וְהַצְלָחָה, בְּרָכָה וִישׁוּעָה, נֶחָמָה פַּרְנָסָה וְכַלְכָּלָה וְרַחֲמִים וְחַיִּים וְשָׁלוֹם וְכָל טוֹב וּמִכָּל טוּב לְעוֹלָם אַל יְחַסְּרֵנוּ:

BLESSED are You, God, our God, King of the universe, good God, our Father, our King, our Might, our Creator, our Liberator, our Maker, our Holy One, the Holy One of Jacob, our Shepherd, the Shepherd of Israel, the King who is good and does good to all, each and every day.

He has done good for us, He does good for us, and He will do good for us; He has treated us, He continues treating us, and He will forever treat us with grace, loving-kindness and mercy, relief, rescue and success, blessing and help, consolation, sustenance and nourishment, compassion, life, peace and all goodness; and may He never cause us to lack any good.

הָרַחֲמָן הוּא יִמְלוֹךְ עָלֵינוּ לְעוֹלָם וָעֶד:

May the Compassionate One reign over us forever and ever.

הָרַחֲמָן הוּא יִתְבָּרַךְ בַּשָּׁמַיִם וּבָאָרֶץ:

May the Compassionate One be blessed in heaven and on earth.

הָרַחֲמָן הוּא יִשְׁתַּבַּח לְדוֹר דּוֹרִים וְיִתְפָּאַר בָּנוּ לָעַד וּלְנֵצַח נְצָחִים וְיִתְהַדַּר בָּנוּ לָעַד וּלְעוֹלְמֵי עוֹלָמִים:

May the Compassionate One be praised for all generations, and be glorified in us forever and all eternity, and honored in us forever and ever.

הָרַחֲמָן הוּא יְפַרְנְסֵנוּ בְּכָבוֹד:

May the Compassionate One sustain us with honor.

הָרַחֲמָן הוּא יִשְׁבּוֹר עוֹל גָּלוּת מֵעַל צַוָּארֵנוּ וְהוּא יוֹלִיכֵנוּ קוֹמְמִיּוּת לְאַרְצֵנוּ:

May the Compassionate One break the yoke of exile from our neck, and may He lead us upright to our land.

הָרַחֲמָן הוּא יִשְׁלַח בְּרָכָה מְרֻבָּה בְּבַיִת זֶה וְעַל שֻׁלְחָן זֶה שֶׁאָכַלְנוּ עָלָיו:

May the Compassionate One send abundant blessing into this house and upon this table at which we have eaten.

If it's Friday night, add the following in honor of Shabbat:

רְצֵה וְהַחֲלִיצֵנוּ יְיָ אֱלֹהֵינוּ בְּמִצְוֹתֶיךָ וּבְמִצְוַת יוֹם הַשְּׁבִיעִי הַשַּׁבָּת הַגָּדוֹל וְהַקָּדוֹשׁ הַזֶּה כִּי יוֹם זֶה גָּדוֹל וְקָדוֹשׁ הוּא לְפָנֶיךָ, לִשְׁבָּת בּוֹ וְלָנוּחַ בּוֹ בְּאַהֲבָה כְּמִצְוַת רְצוֹנֶךָ, וּבִרְצוֹנְךָ הָנִיחַ לָנוּ יְיָ אֱלֹהֵינוּ שֶׁלֹּא תְהֵא צָרָה וְיָגוֹן וַאֲנָחָה בְּיוֹם מְנוּחָתֵנוּ, וְהַרְאֵנוּ יְיָ אֱלֹהֵינוּ בְּנֶחָמַת צִיּוֹן עִירֶךָ, וּבְבִנְיַן יְרוּשָׁלַיִם עִיר קָדְשֶׁךָ, כִּי אַתָּה הוּא בַּעַל הַיְשׁוּעוֹת וּבַעַל הַנֶּחָמוֹת:

MAY it please You, God, our God, to strengthen us through Your commandments, and through the mitzvah of the Seventh Day, this great and holy Shabbat. For this day is great and holy before You, a day to refrain from work and a day when we rest with love, in accordance with the mitzvah You desire. So you should also want, God, our God, to let us have tranquility, so that there shall be no trouble, sadness or grief on the day of our rest. God, our God, let us see the consolation of Zion Your city, and the rebuilding of Jerusalem Your holy city, for You are the Master of liberations and the Master of consolations.

אֱלֹהֵינוּ וֵאלֹהֵי אֲבוֹתֵינוּ, יַעֲלֶה וְיָבֹא וְיַגִּיעַ, וְיֵרָאֶה וְיֵרָצֶה וְיִשָּׁמַע, וְיִפָּקֵד וְיִזָּכֵר זִכְרוֹנֵנוּ וּפִקְדוֹנֵנוּ, וְזִכְרוֹן אֲבוֹתֵינוּ, וְזִכְרוֹן מָשִׁיחַ בֶּן דָּוִד עַבְדֶּךָ, וְזִכְרוֹן יְרוּשָׁלַיִם עִיר קָדְשֶׁךָ, וְזִכְרוֹן כָּל עַמְּךָ בֵּית יִשְׂרָאֵל לְפָנֶיךָ, לִפְלֵיטָה לְטוֹבָה, לְחֵן וּלְחֶסֶד וּלְרַחֲמִים וּלְחַיִּים טוֹבִים וּלְשָׁלוֹם, בְּיוֹם חַג הַמַּצּוֹת הַזֶּה, בְּיוֹם טוֹב מִקְרָא קֹדֶשׁ הַזֶּה, זָכְרֵנוּ יְיָ אֱלֹהֵינוּ בּוֹ לְטוֹבָה (אָמֵן), וּפָקְדֵנוּ בוֹ לִבְרָכָה (אָמֵן), וְהוֹשִׁיעֵנוּ בוֹ לְחַיִּים טוֹבִים (אָמֵן), וּבִדְבַר יְשׁוּעָה וְרַחֲמִים, חוּס וְחָנֵּנוּ, וְרַחֵם עָלֵינוּ וְהוֹשִׁיעֵנוּ, כִּי אֵלֶיךָ עֵינֵינוּ, כִּי אֵל מֶלֶךְ חַנּוּן וְרַחוּם אָתָּה:

OUR God and God of our fathers, may there ascend, come and reach, be seen and accepted, heard, recalled and remembered before You, the remembrance and recollection of us, the remembrance of our fathers, the remembrance of Moshiach the son of David Your servant, the remembrance of Jerusalem Your holy city, and the remembrance of all Your people the House of Israel, for deliverance, wellbeing, grace, loving-kindness, mercy, good life and peace, on this day of the Festival of Matzot, on this day that is considered holy. Remember us on this day, God our God, for good (Amen); recollect us on this day for blessing (Amen); help us on this day for good life (Amen). With the promise of deliverance and compassion, spare us and be gracious to us; have compassion for us and deliver us; for our eyes are directed to You, for You, God, are a gracious and merciful king.

וּבְנֵה יְרוּשָׁלַיִם עִיר הַקֹּדֶשׁ בִּמְהֵרָה בְיָמֵינוּ. בָּרוּךְ אַתָּה יְיָ, בּוֹנֵה בְרַחֲמָיו יְרוּשָׁלָיִם. אָמֵן:

AND rebuild Jerusalem the holy city speedily in our days. Blessed are You, God, who in His mercy rebuilds Jerusalem. Amen.

 You may put your cup down.

Blessing Two

נוֹדֶה לְךָ יְיָ אֱלֹהֵינוּ עַל שֶׁהִנְחַלְתָּ לַאֲבוֹתֵינוּ אֶרֶץ חֶמְדָּה טוֹבָה וּרְחָבָה וְעַל שֶׁהוֹצֵאתָנוּ יְיָ אֱלֹהֵינוּ מֵאֶרֶץ מִצְרַיִם וּפְדִיתָנוּ מִבֵּית עֲבָדִים וְעַל בְּרִיתְךָ שֶׁחָתַמְתָּ בִּבְשָׂרֵנוּ וְעַל תּוֹרָתְךָ שֶׁלִּמַּדְתָּנוּ וְעַל חֻקֶּיךָ שֶׁהוֹדַעְתָּנוּ וְעַל חַיִּים חֵן וָחֶסֶד שֶׁחוֹנַנְתָּנוּ וְעַל אֲכִילַת מָזוֹן שָׁאַתָּה זָן וּמְפַרְנֵס אוֹתָנוּ תָּמִיד בְּכָל יוֹם וּבְכָל עֵת וּבְכָל שָׁעָה:

WE thank You, God, our God, for having given a heritage to our fathers of a precious, good and spacious land; for having brought us out, God our God, out of the land of Egypt and liberating us from slavery; for Your covenant that You have sealed in our flesh; for Your Torah which You have taught us; for Your statutes which You have told us; for the life, favor and loving-kindness which You have graciously bestowed upon us; and for our capacity to eat the food You constantly provide and sustain us with every day, at all times, and at every hour.

וְעַל הַכֹּל יְיָ אֱלֹהֵינוּ אֲנַחְנוּ מוֹדִים לָךְ וּמְבָרְכִים אוֹתָךְ יִתְבָּרַךְ שִׁמְךָ בְּפִי כָּל חַי תָּמִיד לְעוֹלָם וָעֶד, כַּכָּתוּב: וְאָכַלְתָּ וְשָׂבָעְתָּ וּבֵרַכְתָּ אֶת יְיָ אֱלֹהֶיךָ עַל הָאָרֶץ הַטֹּבָה אֲשֶׁר נָתַן לָךְ: בָּרוּךְ אַתָּה יְיָ, עַל הָאָרֶץ וְעַל הַמָּזוֹן:

FOR all this, God our God, we thank You and bless You. May Your reputation be blessed by the mouth of every living being, constantly and forever. As it is written: When you have eaten and are satiated, you shall bless God your God for the good land which He has given you. Blessed are You, God, for the land and for the food.

Blessing Three

רַחֵם יְיָ אֱלֹהֵינוּ עַל יִשְׂרָאֵל עַמֶּךָ וְעַל יְרוּשָׁלַיִם עִירֶךָ וְעַל צִיּוֹן מִשְׁכַּן כְּבוֹדֶךָ וְעַל מַלְכוּת בֵּית דָּוִד מְשִׁיחֶךָ וְעַל הַבַּיִת הַגָּדוֹל וְהַקָּדוֹשׁ שֶׁנִּקְרָא שִׁמְךָ עָלָיו: אֱלֹהֵינוּ אָבִינוּ רוֹעֵנוּ זוֹנֵנוּ פַּרְנְסֵנוּ וְכַלְכְּלֵנוּ וְהַרְוִיחֵנוּ וְהַרְוַח לָנוּ יְיָ אֱלֹהֵינוּ מְהֵרָה מִכָּל צָרוֹתֵינוּ: וְנָא אַל תַּצְרִיכֵנוּ יְיָ אֱלֹהֵינוּ, לֹא לִידֵי מַתְּנַת בָּשָׂר וָדָם וְלֹא לִידֵי הַלְוָאָתָם כִּי אִם לְיָדְךָ הַמְּלֵאָה הַפְּתוּחָה הַקְּדוֹשָׁה וְהָרְחָבָה שֶׁלֹּא נֵבוֹשׁ וְלֹא נִכָּלֵם לְעוֹלָם וָעֶד:

HAVE mercy, God our God, on Israel Your people, on Jerusalem Your city, on Zion the abode of Your glory, on the rule of the house of David Your anointed, and on the great and holy Temple which is called by Your Name.

Our God, our father, our shepherd, feed us, sustain us, nourish us and give us comfort; and speedily, God our God, grant us relief from all our afflictions.

God, our God, please do not make us dependent upon the gifts of mortal men nor upon their loans, but only upon Your full, open, holy and generous hand, that we may not be shamed or disgraced forever and ever.

ברכת המזון
Blessing After the Meal

Blessing One

Now, everyone says together (better: sings together):

Everyone:

בָּרוּךְ אַתָּה יְיָ אֱלֹהֵינוּ מֶלֶךְ הָעוֹלָם, הַזָּן אֶת הָעוֹלָם כֻּלּוֹ בְּטוּבוֹ בְּחֵן בְּחֶסֶד וּבְרַחֲמִים הוּא נוֹתֵן לֶחֶם לְכָל בָּשָׂר כִּי לְעוֹלָם חַסְדּוֹ: וּבְטוּבוֹ הַגָּדוֹל עִמָּנוּ תָּמִיד לֹא חָסַר לָנוּ וְאַל יֶחְסַר לָנוּ מָזוֹן לְעוֹלָם וָעֶד: בַּעֲבוּר שְׁמוֹ הַגָּדוֹל כִּי הוּא אֵל זָן וּמְפַרְנֵס לַכֹּל וּמֵטִיב לַכֹּל וּמֵכִין מָזוֹן לְכָל בְּרִיּוֹתָיו אֲשֶׁר בָּרָא, כָּאָמוּר: פּוֹתֵחַ אֶת יָדֶךָ וּמַשְׂבִּיעַ לְכָל חַי רָצוֹן: בָּרוּךְ אַתָּה יְיָ, הַזָּן אֶת הַכֹּל:

BLESSED are You, God, our God, King of the universe, who, in His goodness, feeds the whole world with grace, with kindness and with mercy.

He gives food to all living creatures, because His loving-kindness is infinite. Through His great goodness to us we never lack food, and may we never lack it, for the sake of His good reputation. For He is a kind God who feeds and sustains all, does good to all, and prepares food for all His creatures whom He has created, as it is said: You open Your hand and satisfy the desire of every living thing. Blessed are You, God, who provides food for all.

**Bah-rookh ah-tah ah-doh-noi eh-loh-hay-noo meh-lekh hah-oh-lahm
hah-zahn eht hah-oh-lahm koo-loh beh-too-voh beh-khayn
beh-kheh-sehd oo-veh-rah-khah-meem
hoo noh-tayn leh-khehm leh-khohl bah-sahr kee leh-oh-lahm khahs-doh.
Oov-too-voh hah-gah-dohl ee-mah-noo tah-meed loh khah-sayr lah-noo
Veh-ahl yekh-sahr lah-noo mah-zohn leh-oh-lahm vah-ehd
Bah-ah-voor sheh-moh hah-gah-dohl kee hoo ayl zahn oo-meh-fahr-nays lah-kohl
oo-may-teev lah-kohl oo-may-kheen mah-zohn leh-khol beh-ree-yoh-tahv
ah-shehr bah-rah, kah-ah-moor poh-tay-ahkh eht yah-deh-khah oo-mahs-bee-ah
leh-khohl khai rah-tzohn, bah-rookh ah-tah ah-doh-noi hah-zahn et hah-kohl.**

Hold your cup until the conclusion of blessing three.

When there are three or more males ages 13 or older, continue with the Zimun, otherwise, continue on next page.

Zimun

Leader: The leader begins:

רַבּוֹתַי מִיר וֶועלִין בֶּענְטשִׁין:

EVERYONE, let's *bentch*!

Rah-boi-sai meer veh-lehn behn-tchehn

Everyone/Leader: The others respond:

יְהִי שֵׁם יְיָ מְבֹרָךְ מֵעַתָּה וְעַד עוֹלָם:

MAY the Name of God be blessed from now and forever.

Yeh-hee shaym ah-doh-noi meh-voh-rahkh may-ah-tah veh-ahd oh-lahm!

Leader: The leader repeats the response. Then he continues:
(If there are 10 or more males over age 13, add the words in parentheses):

בִּרְשׁוּת מָרָנָן וְרַבָּנָן וְרַבּוֹתַי נְבָרֵךְ (אֱלֹהֵינוּ) שֶׁאָכַלְנוּ מִשֶּׁלוֹ:

WITH your permission, masters, teachers and esteemed company,

Let us bless Him (our God) of whose bounty we have eaten.

Bir-shoot mah-rah-nahn veh-rah-bah-nahn veh-rah-boh-tai. Neh-vah-raykh (eh-loh-hay-noo) sheh-ah-khal-noo mee-sheh-loh!

Everyone: The others respond:

בָּרוּךְ (אֱלֹהֵינוּ) שֶׁאָכַלְנוּ מִשֶּׁלוֹ וּבְטוּבוֹ חָיִינוּ:

BLESSED be He (our God) of whose bounty we have eaten and by whose goodness we live.

Bah-rookh (eh-loh-hay-noo) sheh-ah-khal-noo mee-sheh-loh oo-veh-too-voh khah-yee-noo!

Leader: The leader responds:

בָּרוּךְ (אֱלֹהֵינוּ) שֶׁאָכַלְנוּ מִשֶּׁלוֹ וּבְטוּבוֹ חָיִינוּ:

BLESSED be He (our God) of whose bounty we have eaten and by whose goodness we live.

Bah-rookh (eh-loh-hay-noo) sheh-ah-khal-noo mee-sheh-loh oo-veh-too-voh khah-yee-noo!

לִבְנֵי קֹרַח מִזְמוֹר שִׁיר, יְסוּדָתוֹ בְּהַרְרֵי קֹדֶשׁ: אֹהֵב יְיָ שַׁעֲרֵי צִיּוֹן, מִכֹּל מִשְׁכְּנוֹת יַעֲקֹב: נִכְבָּדוֹת מְדֻבָּר בָּךְ, עִיר הָאֱלֹהִים סֶלָה: אַזְכִּיר רַהַב וּבָבֶל לְיֹדְעָי, הִנֵּה פְלֶשֶׁת וְצֹר עִם כּוּשׁ, זֶה יֻלַּד שָׁם: וּלְצִיּוֹן יֵאָמַר אִישׁ וְאִישׁ יֻלַּד בָּהּ, וְהוּא יְכוֹנְנֶהָ עֶלְיוֹן: יְיָ יִסְפֹּר בִּכְתוֹב עַמִּים, זֶה יֻלַּד שָׁם סֶלָה: וְשָׁרִים כְּחֹלְלִים, כָּל מַעְיָנַי בָּךְ:

A PSALM by the sons of Korach:

A song whose foundation is in the holy mountains.

God loves the gates of Zion more than all the dwelling places of Jacob. Glorious things are spoken of you, O city of God.

I will make mention of Rahab and Babylon unto those that know me; behold Philistia and Tyre, as well as Cush, "This one was born there." But of Zion it will be said, "Each one of us was born there," and He, the Most High, will establish it. God will count the register of the nations, "This one was born there." Selah. Singers and dancers alike will chant, "All my inner thoughts are of you."

אֲבָרְכָה אֶת יְיָ בְּכָל עֵת, תָּמִיד תְּהִלָּתוֹ בְּפִי: סוֹף דָּבָר הַכֹּל נִשְׁמָע, אֶת הָאֱלֹהִים יְרָא וְאֶת מִצְוֹתָיו שְׁמוֹר כִּי זֶה כָּל הָאָדָם: תְּהִלַּת יְיָ יְדַבֶּר פִּי וִיבָרֵךְ כָּל בָּשָׂר שֵׁם קָדְשׁוֹ לְעוֹלָם וָעֶד: וַאֲנַחְנוּ נְבָרֵךְ יָהּ מֵעַתָּה וְעַד עוֹלָם הַלְלוּיָהּ:

I WILL BLESS God at all times; His praise is always in my mouth. The ultimate conclusion, all having been heard: Be in awe of God and observe His mitzvahs, for this is what we are all about. My mouth will utter the praise of God, and all living creatures shall bless His holy Name infinitely.

And we will bless God from now and forever; Halleluyah!

At this point we wash the tips of our fingers, at the table, with just a small amount of water.

Before washing your fingertips, say:

זֶה חֵלֶק אָדָם רָשָׁע מֵאֱלֹהִים וְנַחֲלַת אִמְרוֹ מֵאֵל:

THIS is the wicked man's portion from God, and the lot assigned to him by God.

Wash your fingertips, then say:

וַיְדַבֵּר אֵלַי זֶה הַשֻּׁלְחָן אֲשֶׁר לִפְנֵי יְיָ:

HE said to me, "This is the table before God."

Preliminary Psalms

These Psalms are an introduction to *Birkat Hamazon*. The actual blessings begin after this.

Everyone (you can read this quietly):

שִׁיר הַמַּעֲלוֹת, בְּשׁוּב יְיָ אֶת שִׁיבַת צִיּוֹן, הָיִינוּ כְּחֹלְמִים: אָז יִמָּלֵא שְׂחוֹק פִּינוּ וּלְשׁוֹנֵנוּ רִנָּה, אָז יֹאמְרוּ בַגּוֹיִם, הִגְדִּיל יְיָ לַעֲשׂוֹת עִם אֵלֶּה: הִגְדִּיל יְיָ לַעֲשׂוֹת עִמָּנוּ, הָיִינוּ שְׂמֵחִים: שׁוּבָה יְיָ אֶת שְׁבִיתֵנוּ, כַּאֲפִיקִים בַּנֶּגֶב: הַזֹּרְעִים בְּדִמְעָה, בְּרִנָּה יִקְצֹרוּ: הָלוֹךְ יֵלֵךְ וּבָכֹה נֹשֵׂא מֶשֶׁךְ הַזָּרַע, בֹּא יָבֹא בְרִנָּה נֹשֵׂא אֲלֻמֹּתָיו:

A Song for Rising Higher:

When God will begin to bring back the exiles of Zion (that's us), we will discover we were like dreamers.

Right away, our mouths will fill with laughter, our tongues with happy songs.

Then the nations of the world will be so astonished, they will say, "God is doing great things for these people!"

"True," we will respond, "God is about to do some great things for us!" And we will start celebrating right away.

"Oh God!" we will say. "Bring our exiles home right away, like the rapid streams of a Negev rainstorm that suddenly transform it to moist, fertile soil!"

And He will respond, "Yes! Now that they've finished seeding, those who have sown with tears will reap the fruit of their planting with joyous song."

"Those who journey up and down the fields of exile, weeping with their seeding tools, they will come back, come back with joyous song, carrying their sheaves."

בָּרֵךְ Beirach

Thank God for the Meal

Once everyone's done with the matzah, it's time to thank God for the food. Jews call this *Birkat Hamazon*, or "*bentching*."

THE TORAH SAYS that when we "have eaten and are satiated" we should show some gratitude. We do that with four blessings—and there's a history behind them:

Moses provided the first blessing in gratitude for the manna that fell from heaven. Joshua composed a second blessing for the Land of Israel. King David composed the third for the city of Jerusalem, our eternal capital.

The fourth was added in Roman times, and is followed by a series of petitions that were added a bit later.

Pour the Third Cup

First, everyone fills their cup again with wine. This is the third cup, and we'll be drinking it right after we finish *Birkat Hamazon*.

Some pour a special cup for Elijah the Prophet now. Others do that after *Birkat Hamazon*.

POURING THE THIRD CUP marks a major shift in the Seder. Until now, the Seder was principally about the past. Now we start moving to the future.

Like we explained at the beginning of the Seder, the four cups correspond to: Extract, Rescue, Liberate, Marry. So now we're at the Liberate stage.

The real liberation doesn't totally kick in until the final Messianic Era, which will start with a public announcement from Elijah the Prophet.

We want Elijah to feel at home when he comes in, so we pour a cup for him now (or before the fourth cup).

שֻׁלְחָן עוֹרֵךְ Shulchan Orech
A Festive Meal

Eat food!

You can also eat the egg from the Seder plate now, dipped in saltwater. No blessing on that.

Remember to leave room for more matzah at the end!

Try to get to the next step before midnight (at least on the first night of Passover). (Midnight is not necessarily 12 AM. Consult your local Jewish calendar for the time in your location.)

צָפוּן Tzafun
Eat the Afikoman

Remember the piece of matzah you broke off and put aside? Now that you've finished the meal, it's time to make sure everyone gets a piece of that to eat.

This matzah is in place of the Passover lamb, and that was always the last thing eaten in the meal.

You'll need to supplement it with any other matzah lying around to make sure everyone eats at least one quarter of a typical shmurah matzah, or half a machine matzah. Even better if you can eat double that amount.

> Eat the matzah you hid at the beginning of the Seder while leaning. Don't eat anything else after this.

After this, we don't eat anything, so that we leave the Seder with the taste of matzah in our mouths.

 Korech

Bitter Leaves in a Wrapping

 SOME PEOPLE THINK we do this because the Children of Israel packed sandwiches when they left Egypt. But that's not so.

It all goes back to the period when the Second Temple was still in operation in Jerusalem. So they were still eating the Passover lamb offering.

A wise elder named Hillel, head of the Supreme Court at the time, determined that the Passover meat, the matzah and the *maror* were all supposed to be eaten together, as a sandwich. The other sages disagreed, saying you could eat them separately.

As often occurs between wise people, each side had a good point, and their disagreement was never resolved. So, to this day, we follow both opinions.

Which goes to show that two different opinions can both be right. Indeed, in a similar situation, a heavenly voice proclaimed, "Both are the words of the living God!"

Take some matzah from the bottom matzah, or somewhere else if there's none left. Same amount as you used before—at least a quarter of a shmurah matzah or half a machine matzah.

Now dip some of those bitter chazeret greens in the charoset. Use the same amount you used last time. Place it together with your matzah in whatever sandwich-wrap fashion you like.

(If you are careful about not getting matzah wet, dry off the chazeret first. Also, use dry charoset.)

Now say:

 Everyone:

כֵּן עָשָׂה הִלֵּל בִּזְמַן שֶׁבֵּית הַמִּקְדָּשׁ הָיָה קַיָּם, הָיָה כּוֹרֵךְ פֶּסַח מַצָּה וּמָרוֹר וְאוֹכֵל בְּיַחַד, כְּמוֹ שֶׁנֶּאֱמַר: עַל מַצּוֹת וּמְרוֹרִים יֹאכְלֻהוּ:

THIS is what Hillel did in the time when the Temple was standing.

He would wrap Pesach, Matzah and Maror and eat them together, just like it says, "On matzah and bitter herbs they will eat it."

Now lean to your left and eat!

 מָרוֹר Maror

Bitter Leaves for Eating

After you've given everyone enough time for that totally awesome mitzvah-eating ceremony, we get yet another one. This time, however, you don't lean.

 IN THE TORAH, God tells Moses to tell us to eat the Passover offering with matzah and a bitter vegetable. That way, we will remember the bitterness of Egyptian persecution.

Since it's something God told us to do, that makes it a mitzvah. Since we don't have a Passover offering these days, that makes it no longer a mitzvah. But since the sages of the Talmud instructed us to continue doing it nonetheless, so it won't be forgotten, that makes it a mitzvah again—a rabbinic mitzvah.

Because the Torah says to listen to the sages.

Everyone takes just over half an ounce (17 grams) of maror (or more if they want) and dips it in the charoset. Then, say this blessing:

 Everyone:

בָּרוּךְ אַתָּה יְיָ, אֱלֹהֵינוּ מֶלֶךְ הָעוֹלָם, אֲשֶׁר קִדְּשָׁנוּ בְּמִצְוֹתָיו, וְצִוָּנוּ עַל אֲכִילַת מָרוֹר:

BLESSED are You, God, our God, King of the universe, who has made us holy with His mitzvahs, and commanded us concerning eating a bitter vegetable.

Bah-rookh ah-tah ah-doh-noi eh-loh-hay-noo meh-lekh hah-oh-lahm ah-sher ki-deh-shah-noo beh-mitz-voh-tahv veh-tzee-vah-noo ahl ah-khee-laht mah-rohr.

Don't lean while you eat the *maror*.

Blessing on Matzah

Pick up the matzahs—all three of them. Say the blessing that we always say on bread. (Matzah, after all, is also bread—just that it didn't get a chance to rise.)

Everyone

בָּרוּךְ אַתָּה יְיָ, אֱלֹהֵינוּ מֶלֶךְ הָעוֹלָם, הַמּוֹצִיא לֶחֶם מִן הָאָרֶץ:

BLESSED are You, God, our God, King of the universe, who brings bread out of the earth.

Bah-rookh ah-tah ah-doh-noi eh-loh-hay-noo meh-lekh hah-oh-lahm hah-moh-tzee leh-khehm min hah-ah-rehtz.

No, don't eat it yet. That was the blessing on the bread. Now comes the blessing on the opportunity to do this mitzvah.

Blessing on the Mitzvah

Release the bottom matzah. Holding the top two matzahs, say this blessing:

Everyone

בָּרוּךְ אַתָּה יְיָ, אֱלֹהֵינוּ מֶלֶךְ הָעוֹלָם, אֲשֶׁר קִדְּשָׁנוּ בְּמִצְוֹתָיו, וְצִוָּנוּ עַל אֲכִילַת מַצָּה:

BLESSED are You, God, our God, King of the universe, who has made us holy with His mitzvahs, and commanded us concerning eating matzah.

Bah-rookh ah-tah ah-doh-noi eh-loh-hay-noo meh-lekh hah-oh-lahm ah-sher ki-deh-shah-noo beh-mitz-voh-tahv veh-tzee-vah-noo ahl ah-khee-laht mah-tzah.

Now everyone leans to their left and eats matzah.

Make sure to eat at least a quarter of a typical shmurah matzah, or half a machine matzah. If you are eating from your own Seder plate, with your own set of three matzahs, best to eat that amount twice—one portion from the middle matzah, one from the top matzah.

Rachtza

Wash Hands with a Blessing

Stop and read this before you go further. We're about to do the matzah thing, and it ain't simple.

This is what's going to happen now: We're about to eat a mitzvah. Generally, you just do mitzvahs. But, until the Temple is rebuilt, this is the only opportunity in the year that we get to actually eat a Biblical mitzvah. Now that's neat. You're going to have body cells made out of something Godly.

We're going to eat it while leaning to the left, just like when we drank the wine. That's to show that we are free, and free people don't have to sit up straight when they eat.

And we're going to eat a sizable amount of it. Like at least a quarter of a hand-baked matzah, or half a machine-baked matzah. If there's not enough in the top two matzahs to give everyone enough to eat, you'll need to supplement it with some more matzah from somewhere else. Just make sure everyone gets a little from the Seder plate matzah you're making the blessing over.

So now let's start:

Remember the hand-washing ritual at the beginning of the Seder? Well, we're doing it again.

Pour water on each hand three times using a washing cup, covering the entire hand each time, from the wrist to the fingertips. This time, say a blessing:

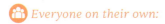
Everyone on their own:

בָּרוּךְ אַתָּה יְיָ, אֱלֹהֵינוּ מֶלֶךְ הָעוֹלָם, אֲשֶׁר קִדְּשָׁנוּ בְּמִצְוֹתָיו, וְצִוָּנוּ עַל נְטִילַת יָדָיִם:

BLESSED are You, God, our God, King of the universe, who has made us holy with His mitzvahs, and commanded us concerning washing hands.

Bah-rookh ah-tah ah-doh-noi eh-loh-hay-noo meh-lekh hah-oh-lahm ah-sher ki-deh-shah-noo beh-mitz-voh-tahv veh-tzee-vah-noo ahl neh-tee-laht yah-dah-yim.

Now dry your hands and return to your seats. No conversation until the matzah's been eaten.

Pick up those cups again.

 Everyone:

MAGID

בָּרוּךְ אַתָּה יְיָ, אֱלֹהֵינוּ מֶלֶךְ הָעוֹלָם, אֲשֶׁר גְּאָלָנוּ וְגָאַל אֶת אֲבוֹתֵינוּ מִמִּצְרַיִם, וְהִגִּיעָנוּ הַלַּיְלָה הַזֶּה לֶאֱכָל בּוֹ מַצָּה וּמָרוֹר. כֵּן יְיָ אֱלֹהֵינוּ וֵאלֹהֵי אֲבוֹתֵינוּ יַגִּיעֵנוּ לְמוֹעֲדִים וְלִרְגָלִים אֲחֵרִים הַבָּאִים לִקְרָאתֵנוּ לְשָׁלוֹם, שְׂמֵחִים בְּבִנְיַן עִירֶךָ, וְשָׂשִׂים בַּעֲבוֹדָתֶךָ,

BLESSED are You, God, our God, King of the universe, who has liberated us and liberated our fathers from Egypt, and got us all the way to this night to eat matzah and maror.

So too, God, our God and God of our fathers, get us all the way to the other holidays and festivals that are coming to greet us in peace, celebrating in the rebuilding of Your city, and rejoicing in Your service.

When the Seder is on Saturday night, say:

וְנֹאכַל שָׁם מִן הַפְּסָחִים וּמִן הַזְּבָחִים

Then we shall eat of the Pesach-offerings and of the sacrifices...

When the Seder is on any night other than Saturday night:

וְנֹאכַל שָׁם מִן הַזְּבָחִים וּמִן הַפְּסָחִים

Then we shall eat of the sacrifices and of the Pesach-offerings...

Continue:

אֲשֶׁר יַגִּיעַ דָּמָם עַל קִיר מִזְבַּחֲךָ לְרָצוֹן, וְנוֹדֶה לְךָ שִׁיר חָדָשׁ עַל גְּאֻלָּתֵנוּ וְעַל פְּדוּת נַפְשֵׁנוּ. בָּרוּךְ אַתָּה יְיָ, גָּאַל יִשְׂרָאֵל:

...whose blood shall be sprinkled on the wall of Your altar for acceptance; and we shall thank You with a new song for our liberation and for the rescue of our souls. Blessed are You, God, who liberated Israel.

בָּרוּךְ אַתָּה יְיָ, אֱלֹהֵינוּ מֶלֶךְ הָעוֹלָם, בּוֹרֵא פְּרִי הַגָּפֶן:

BLESSED are You, God, our God, King of the universe, who creates the fruit of the vine.

Bah-rookh ah-tah ah-doh-noi eh-loh-hay-noo meh-lekh hah-oh-lahm boh-ray pree hah-gah-fehn.

② Now lean to the left and drink your entire second cup of wine—or at least most of it.

הַלְלוּיָהּ

הַֽלְלוּ עַבְדֵי יְיָ, הַֽלְלוּ אֶת שֵׁם יְיָ: יְהִי שֵׁם יְיָ מְבֹרָךְ, מֵעַתָּה וְעַד עוֹלָם: מִמִּזְרַח שֶׁמֶשׁ עַד מְבוֹאוֹ, מְהֻלָּל שֵׁם יְיָ: רָם עַל כָּל גּוֹיִם יְיָ, עַל הַשָּׁמַיִם כְּבוֹדוֹ: מִי כַּיְיָ אֱלֹהֵינוּ, הַמַּגְבִּיהִי לָשָֽׁבֶת: הַמַּשְׁפִּילִי לִרְאוֹת, בַּשָּׁמַיִם וּבָאָֽרֶץ: מְקִימִי מֵעָפָר דָּל, מֵאַשְׁפֹּת יָרִים אֶבְיוֹן: לְהוֹשִׁיבִי עִם נְדִיבִים, עִם נְדִיבֵי עַמּוֹ: מֽוֹשִׁיבִי עֲקֶֽרֶת הַבַּֽיִת, אֵם הַבָּנִים שְׂמֵחָה, הַֽלְלוּיָהּ:

HALLELUYAH!

Offer praise, you servants of God! praise the name of God.

May God's name be blessed now and forever.

From sunrise to sunset, God's name is praised.

God is way beyond anything people of this world could imagine, way beyond anything the heavenly beings can imagine.

Who is like God our God, who dwells on high yet looks down so low upon heaven and earth!

He raises the poor from the dust, He lifts the needy from the trash, to seat them with the major donors, with the benefactors of His people.

He transforms the barren woman to a family woman, into a joyful mother of children.

Halleluyah!

בְּצֵאת

יִשְׂרָאֵל מִמִּצְרָֽיִם, בֵּית יַעֲקֹב מֵעַם לֹעֵז: הָיְתָה יְהוּדָה לְקָדְשׁוֹ, יִשְׂרָאֵל מַמְשְׁלוֹתָיו: הַיָּם רָאָה וַיָּנֹס, הַיַּרְדֵּן יִסֹּב לְאָחוֹר: הֶהָרִים רָקְדוּ כְאֵילִים, גְּבָעוֹת כִּבְנֵי צֹאן: מַה לְּךָ הַיָּם כִּי תָנוּס, הַיַּרְדֵּן תִּסֹּב לְאָחוֹר: הֶהָרִים תִּרְקְדוּ כְאֵילִים, גְּבָעוֹת כִּבְנֵי צֹאן: מִלִּפְנֵי אָדוֹן חֽוּלִי אָֽרֶץ, מִלִּפְנֵי אֱלֽוֹהַּ יַעֲקֹב: הַהֹפְכִי הַצּוּר אֲגַם מָֽיִם, חַלָּמִישׁ לְמַעְיְנוֹ מָֽיִם:

WHEN Israel went out of Egypt, the House of Jacob from a people of a foreign language, Judah became His holy one, Israel His dominion.

The sea saw and split, the Jordan turned back on itself. The mountains skipped like rams, the hills like young sheep.

What is with you, O sea, that you split? Jordan, that you turn back on yourself?

Mountains, why do you skip like rams; hills, like lambs?

They all answer, "Before the Master, He who bore the earth! Before the God of Jacob!

"He turns hard rock into a pool of water! A flintstone into a spring of water!"

In First Person

 Someone out loud:

בְּכָל דּוֹר וָדוֹר חַיָּב אָדָם לִרְאוֹת אֶת עַצְמוֹ כְּאִלּוּ הוּא יָצָא מִמִּצְרַיִם, שֶׁנֶּאֱמַר: וְהִגַּדְתָּ לְבִנְךָ בַּיּוֹם הַהוּא לֵאמֹר בַּעֲבוּר זֶה עָשָׂה יְיָ לִי בְּצֵאתִי מִמִּצְרָיִם: לֹא אֶת אֲבוֹתֵינוּ בִּלְבַד גָּאַל הַקָּדוֹשׁ בָּרוּךְ הוּא מִמִּצְרַיִם, אֶלָּא אַף אוֹתָנוּ גָּאַל עִמָּהֶם, שֶׁנֶּאֱמַר: וְאוֹתָנוּ הוֹצִיא מִשָּׁם לְמַעַן הָבִיא אוֹתָנוּ לָתֶת לָנוּ אֶת הָאָרֶץ אֲשֶׁר נִשְׁבַּע לַאֲבוֹתֵינוּ:

IN every single generation, every person has to see him or herself as though he or she actually left Egypt. That's what it says:

"And you shall tell the story to your child on that day, saying, 'So that I would do all this Seder and tell this story—that's why God did all that for me when I left Egypt.'"

It wasn't just our ancestors that the Holy One Blessed Be He liberated from Egypt—He liberated us along with them. Like it says:

"It was us that He took out from there, so that He could bring us here, to give us the land that He promised to our ancestors."

> **THE EGYPTIANS** ruled over our bodies and our spirits. When we left Egypt, our spirits were eternally liberated. Whatever our oppressors inflicted upon us, we always retained the power at any moment to connect to the Infinite, and with a mitzvah, with a prayer, with a few words of Torah, we were free.
>
> That is what a mitzvah is all about—a connection to the Infinite, available at all times, in all places.[43]

Blessing on the Second Cup

 Now we cover the matzah and lift up our cups. And we all say:

 Everyone:

לְפִיכָךְ אֲנַחְנוּ חַיָּבִים: לְהוֹדוֹת לְהַלֵּל לְשַׁבֵּחַ לְפָאֵר לְרוֹמֵם לְהַדֵּר לְבָרֵךְ לְעַלֵּה וּלְקַלֵּס, לְמִי שֶׁעָשָׂה לַאֲבוֹתֵינוּ וְלָנוּ אֶת כָּל הַנִּסִּים הָאֵלּוּ. הוֹצִיאָנוּ מֵעַבְדוּת לְחֵרוּת, מִיָּגוֹן לְשִׂמְחָה, וּמֵאֵבֶל לְיוֹם טוֹב, וּמֵאֲפֵלָה לְאוֹר גָּדוֹל, וּמִשִּׁעְבּוּד לִגְאֻלָּה, וְנֹאמַר לְפָנָיו הַלְלוּיָהּ:

THAT'S why it's up to us to thank, to praise, to rave about, to glorify, to exalt, to acclaim, to bless, to raise up and to pay homage to the One who did all these miracles for our ancestors and for us.

He took us out of slavery to freedom, from misery to joy, from mourning to celebration, from murky darkness to great light, and from oppression to liberation.

So let's give Him some praise, by saying Halleluyah:

 Cups can be put down here for a minute.

Maror

Now put your hand over the maror—that's the bitter vegetables on the plate—and say together:

 Everyone:

מָרוֹר זֶה שֶׁאָנוּ אוֹכְלִים עַל שׁוּם מָה,

THIS bitter vegetable that we eat, what's it all about?

You can take your hand back now.

עַל שׁוּם שֶׁמֵּרְרוּ הַמִּצְרִים אֶת חַיֵּי אֲבוֹתֵינוּ בְּמִצְרָיִם,

שֶׁנֶּאֱמַר: וַיְמָרְרוּ אֶת חַיֵּיהֶם בַּעֲבֹדָה קָשָׁה בְּחֹמֶר וּבִלְבֵנִים וּבְכָל עֲבֹדָה בַּשָּׂדֶה, אֵת כָּל עֲבֹדָתָם אֲשֶׁר עָבְדוּ בָהֶם בְּפָרֶךְ:

It's because the Egyptians embittered the lives of our ancestors in Egypt.

Just like it says in the story:

"They embittered their lives with hard work, with mortar and with bricks and all kinds of field work. Everything they made them do was to break them."

 WHAT IS the most important thing to have at a Seder? A Jew.

The matzah at your table didn't leave Egypt. Neither did the wine or the bitter herbs. The lamb isn't even here. The Jew is the only thing here that's real. The Jew actually left Egypt.

Once he or she is here, the matzah is the matzah that he took with him from Egypt, the bitter herbs are the bitterness of his slavery, the wine is the taste of freedom, and the lamb—we'll have that soon, also.

Matzah

Now hold on to the top two matzahs inside their cloth, and say together:

 Everyone:

מַצָּה זוֹ שֶׁאָנוּ אוֹכְלִים עַל שׁוּם מָה,

THIS matzah that we eat, what's it all about?

You can let go of the matzah at this point.

עַל שׁוּם שֶׁלֹּא הִסְפִּיק בְּצֵקָת שֶׁל אֲבוֹתֵינוּ לְהַחֲמִיץ עַד שֶׁנִּגְלָה עֲלֵיהֶם מֶלֶךְ מַלְכֵי הַמְּלָכִים הַקָּדוֹשׁ בָּרוּךְ הוּא וּגְאָלָם,

It's because the dough of our ancestors hadn't had enough time to rise, when suddenly the King of the kings of kings, the Holy One Blessed Be He, revealed Himself to them and liberated them.

Just like it says in the story:

שֶׁנֶּאֱמַר: וַיֹּאפוּ אֶת הַבָּצֵק אֲשֶׁר הוֹצִיאוּ מִמִּצְרַיִם עֻגֹת מַצּוֹת, כִּי לֹא חָמֵץ, כִּי גֹרְשׁוּ מִמִּצְרַיִם וְלֹא יָכְלוּ לְהִתְמַהְמֵהַּ, וְגַם צֵדָה לֹא עָשׂוּ לָהֶם:

"They baked matzah from the dough that they had brought out of Egypt, because it hadn't become chametz—because they had been chased out of Egypt and didn't have a chance to stick around waiting for the dough to rise. They didn't even have time to pack anything else to eat."

 WE RAN OUT OF EGYPT. We never really internalized what was happening with us. And when you don't internalize your freedom, when it's just something that was handed to you, you're never truly free.

But in Messianic times, we won't have to run. Why? Because that time around, our liberation will have been achieved through our own hard work and suffering over these many years of exile. So it will be real, through and through.

Besides, there won't be anything left to run from. Everything of this world will remain, and it will all be good. Because everything God made is inherently good. It's just left up to us to reveal that good, each one of us, through our own work.[42]

Pesach

 Everyone:

פֶּסַח שֶׁהָיוּ אֲבוֹתֵינוּ אוֹכְלִים בִּזְמַן שֶׁבֵּית הַמִּקְדָּשׁ קַיָּם עַל שׁוּם מָה,

עַל שׁוּם שֶׁפָּסַח הַמָּקוֹם עַל בָּתֵּי אֲבוֹתֵינוּ בְּמִצְרַיִם,

שֶׁנֶּאֱמַר: וַאֲמַרְתֶּם זֶבַח פֶּסַח הוּא לַייָ אֲשֶׁר פָּסַח עַל בָּתֵּי בְנֵי יִשְׂרָאֵל בְּמִצְרַיִם בְּנָגְפּוֹ אֶת מִצְרַיִם וְאֶת בָּתֵּינוּ הִצִּיל, וַיִּקֹּד הָעָם וַיִּשְׁתַּחֲווּ:

THE Pesach is the Passover offering that our ancestors ate in the time when the Holy Temple was standing. What was that all about?

It was because Pesach means to skip over. And the One Who Encompasses Everything skipped over our ancestors' houses in Egypt. When we were about to leave Egypt, Moses told us how to explain eating matzah on Passover to future generations. He said:

"You shall say, 'It is a Pesach offering to God, because He skipped over the houses of the Children of Israel in Egypt when He struck the Egyptians with a plague, and He saved our houses.' And the people bowed and prostrated themselves."

THIS IS WHERE the Exodus storytelling section signs off. But why must the last line of the story be about cleaning up "all our sins"? Especially since that didn't happen until hundreds of years after the Exodus.

And anyways, if we're going to mention the Chosen Temple in Jerusalem, why do we have to harp on the sin thing? How about the fact that God's presence filled that special place?

When you know the inside story of the Exodus, it all makes sense.

The Exodus was meant to heal the Tree of Knowledge affair—when we got booted out of the Garden of Eden. We became slaves to our own egos, which led to becoming slaves to egomaniacs who built empires, and eventually slaves to our credit cards.

The Egypt stint—suffering enslavement and then breaking out of bondage—was meant to heal all that. But the operation was prematurely aborted when the Egyptians went overboard on the oppression stuff. Our souls had to wait until the Temple was built in Jerusalem to complete their rehab.

And since that went haywire as well, the journey of Exodus has continued until now. Until, very soon, as the Third Temple is constructed, all of humanity will experience the ultimate exodus from our ego-bondage. We will finally be back in that Garden of Eden state of being.

But it will be way beyond better this time around, because we won't just be plopped down in there. We will be there through our own choices and hard work. It will be a Chosen Temple—built of our making the right choices.

May that Third and Final Chosen Temple be built sooner than we can imagine.[41]

The Essentials

 Leader:

רַבָּן גַּמְלִיאֵל הָיָה אוֹמֵר: כָּל שֶׁלֹּא אָמַר שְׁלֹשָׁה דְבָרִים אֵלּוּ בַּפֶּסַח לֹא יָצָא יְדֵי חוֹבָתוֹ. וְאֵלּוּ הֵן:

RABBAN Gamliel used to say that anyone who didn't mention the following three things on Passover, didn't really do the Seder right.

 Everyone:

So everyone say together:

Pesach! Matzah!...and Maror!

פֶּסַח, מַצָּה וּמָרוֹר:

 Leader:

Actually, he didn't just mean to mention them. He meant to explain what they're there for. So let's do that. Again, tonight we always start with a question:

Someone out loud:

עַל אַחַת כַּמָּה וְכַמָּה טוֹבָה כְפוּלָה וּמְכֻפֶּלֶת לַמָּקוֹם עָלֵינוּ,

IF so, how much more so should we be grateful to the One Who Encompasses Everything for the doubled and redoubled goodness that He has done for us!

1. שֶׁהוֹצִיאָנוּ מִמִּצְרַיִם, — He brought us out of Egypt
2. וְעָשָׂה בָהֶם שְׁפָטִים, — And He carried out judgments against them
3. וְעָשָׂה בֵאלֹהֵיהֶם, — And He did the same to their idols
4. וְהָרַג אֶת בְּכוֹרֵיהֶם, — And He struck their firstborn
5. וְנָתַן לָנוּ אֶת מָמוֹנָם, — And He gave us their belongings
6. וְקָרַע לָנוּ אֶת הַיָּם, — And He split the sea for us
7. וְהֶעֱבִירָנוּ בְתוֹכוֹ בֶּחָרָבָה, — And He took us through it on dry land
8. וְשִׁקַּע צָרֵינוּ בְּתוֹכוֹ, — And He drowned our oppressors in it
9. וְסִפֵּק צָרְכֵּנוּ בַּמִּדְבָּר אַרְבָּעִים שָׁנָה, — And He supplied our needs in the desert for forty years
10. וְהֶאֱכִילָנוּ אֶת הַמָּן, — And He fed us the manna
11. וְנָתַן לָנוּ אֶת הַשַּׁבָּת, — And He gave us the Shabbat
12. וְקֵרְבָנוּ לִפְנֵי הַר סִינַי, — And He brought us before Mount Sinai
13. וְנָתַן לָנוּ אֶת הַתּוֹרָה, — And He gave us the Torah
14. וְהִכְנִיסָנוּ לְאֶרֶץ יִשְׂרָאֵל, — And He brought us into the land of Israel
15. וּבָנָה לָנוּ אֶת בֵּית הַבְּחִירָה לְכַפֵּר עַל כָּל עֲוֹנוֹתֵינוּ: — And He built the Chosen Temple for us, so we could atone for all we may have done wrong.

אִלּוּ הֶאֱכִילָנוּ אֶת הַמָּן וְלֹא נָתַן לָנוּ אֶת הַשַּׁבָּת, דַּיֵּנוּ:

If He had fed us the manna,
but not given us the Shabbat,
that would have been good enough for us!

אִלּוּ נָתַן לָנוּ אֶת הַשַּׁבָּת וְלֹא קֵרְבָנוּ לִפְנֵי הַר סִינַי, דַּיֵּנוּ:

If He had given us the Shabbat,
but not brought us before Mount Sinai,
that would have been good enough for us!

אִלּוּ קֵרְבָנוּ לִפְנֵי הַר סִינַי וְלֹא נָתַן לָנוּ אֶת הַתּוֹרָה, דַּיֵּנוּ:

If He had brought us to hear and see God speak at Mount Sinai,
but not given us the Torah,
that would have been good enough for us!

אִלּוּ נָתַן לָנוּ אֶת הַתּוֹרָה וְלֹא הִכְנִיסָנוּ לְאֶרֶץ יִשְׂרָאֵל, דַּיֵּנוּ:

If He had given us the Torah,
but not brought us into the land of Israel,
that would have been good enough for us!

אִלּוּ הִכְנִיסָנוּ לְאֶרֶץ יִשְׂרָאֵל וְלֹא בָנָה לָנוּ אֶת בֵּית הַבְּחִירָה, דַּיֵּנוּ:

If He had brought us into the land of Israel,
but not built for us the Chosen Temple,
that would have been good enough for us!

Everyone: You can sing this in the original Hebrew as well. Here's the first stanza:

**Ee-loo hoh-tzee-ah-noo, mee-mitz-rah-yim
veh-loh ah-sah bah-hehm sheh-fah-teem dah-yay-noo!
Ee-loo ah-sah bah-hehm sheh-fah-teem
veh-loh ah-sah vay-loh-hay-hehm dah-yay-noo!**

Showing Appreciation (Dayenu)

 *Someone or Everyone:*

Having counted all the goodness God has done for us, we burst out:[40]

כַּ֫מָּה מַעֲלוֹת טוֹבוֹת לַמָּקוֹם עָלֵינוּ:	Wow! How many levels upon levels of favors did the One Who Encompasses Everything do for us!
אִלּוּ הוֹצִיאָנוּ מִמִּצְרַיִם וְלֹא עָשָׂה בָהֶם שְׁפָטִים, דַּיֵּנוּ:	If He had just brought us out from Egypt, but didn't carry out judgments against them, that would have been good enough for us!
אִלּוּ עָשָׂה בָהֶם שְׁפָטִים וְלֹא עָשָׂה בֵאלֹהֵיהֶם, דַּיֵּנוּ:	If He had carried out judgments against them, but not against their idols, that would have been good enough for us!
אִלּוּ עָשָׂה בֵאלֹהֵיהֶם וְלֹא הָרַג אֶת בְּכוֹרֵיהֶם, דַּיֵּנוּ:	If He had destroyed their idols, but not struck their firstborn, that would have been good enough for us!
אִלּוּ הָרַג אֶת בְּכוֹרֵיהֶם וְלֹא נָתַן לָנוּ אֶת מָמוֹנָם, דַּיֵּנוּ:	If He had struck their firstborn, but not given us their valuables, that would have been good enough for us!
אִלּוּ נָתַן לָנוּ אֶת מָמוֹנָם וְלֹא קָרַע לָנוּ אֶת הַיָּם, דַּיֵּנוּ:	If He had given us their valuables, but not split the sea for us, that would have been good enough for us!
אִלּוּ קָרַע לָנוּ אֶת הַיָּם וְלֹא הֶעֱבִירָנוּ בְּתוֹכוֹ בֶּחָרָבָה, דַּיֵּנוּ:	If He had split the sea for us, but not taken us through it comfortably on dry land, that would have been good enough for us!
אִלּוּ הֶעֱבִירָנוּ בְּתוֹכוֹ בֶּחָרָבָה וְלֹא שִׁקַּע צָרֵינוּ בְּתוֹכוֹ, דַּיֵּנוּ:	If He had taken us through the sea on dry land, but not drowned our oppressors in it, that would have been good enough for us!
אִלּוּ שִׁקַּע צָרֵינוּ בְּתוֹכוֹ וְלֹא סִפֵּק צָרְכֵּנוּ בַּמִּדְבָּר אַרְבָּעִים שָׁנָה, דַּיֵּנוּ:	If He had drowned our oppressors in it, but not supplied our needs in the desert for forty years, that would have been good enough for us!
אִלּוּ סִפֵּק צָרְכֵּנוּ בַּמִּדְבָּר אַרְבָּעִים שָׁנָה וְלֹא הֶאֱכִילָנוּ אֶת הַמָּן, דַּיֵּנוּ:	If He had supplied our needs in the desert for forty years, but not fed us the manna, that would have been good enough for us!

MAGID

 Someone else out loud:

רַבִּי עֲקִיבָא אוֹמֵר: מִנַּיִן שֶׁכָּל מַכָּה וּמַכָּה שֶׁהֵבִיא הַקָּדוֹשׁ בָּרוּךְ הוּא עַל הַמִּצְרִים בְּמִצְרַיִם הָיְתָה שֶׁל חָמֵשׁ מַכּוֹת,

שֶׁנֶּאֱמַר: יְשַׁלַּח בָּם חֲרוֹן אַפּוֹ, עֶבְרָה, וָזַעַם, וְצָרָה, מִשְׁלַחַת מַלְאֲכֵי רָעִים:

חֲרוֹן אַפּוֹ אַחַת, עֶבְרָה שְׁתַּיִם, וָזַעַם שָׁלֹשׁ, וְצָרָה אַרְבַּע, מִשְׁלַחַת מַלְאֲכֵי רָעִים חָמֵשׁ,

אֱמוֹר מֵעַתָּה: בְּמִצְרַיִם לָקוּ חֲמִשִּׁים מַכּוֹת, וְעַל הַיָּם לָקוּ חֲמִשִּׁים וּמָאתַיִם מַכּוֹת:

RABBI Akiva took it even further.

How do we know that each individual plague which God brought upon the Egyptians in Egypt consisted of (not four, but) five plagues?

Well, I'll tell you: Let's go back to how the Psalms describes the plagues:

"He sent against them His fierce anger, fury, wrath, and torment, a dispatch of nasty angels."

Fierce anger is one.

Fury is two.

Wrath makes three.

Torment makes four.

A dispatch of nasty angels makes five.

5 x 10 = 50. So it turns out that in Egypt they were struck by fifty plagues.

50 x 5 = 250. And at the sea they were stricken by 250 plagues!

THE NEED for such a great number of plagues is an indication of how deeply we were held captive by the bad energy of Egypt. All of that had to be flushed out by these plagues before we could be torn out of there. Which is all the more we have to be grateful for.

And that explains why this leads into...

RABBI Yosai (who was from the Galilee) calculated the number of plagues at the splitting of the sea like this:

How do we know that the Egyptians were struck by ten plagues in Egypt, and then were struck by fifty plagues at the splitting of the Sea of Reeds?

Well, I'll tell you: In Egypt, the magicians said to Pharaoh, "This is the finger of God."

And at the sea, it says that "Israel saw the great hand that God laid against Egypt; and the people feared God, and they believed in God and in His servant Moses."

Now, by how many plagues were they struck when they called it "the finger of God"? Ten plagues! Being struck by God's hand must mean five times that, right? So you have to conclude that in Egypt they were struck by ten plagues, but at the sea they were struck by fifty plagues!

רַבִּי יוֹסֵי הַגְּלִילִי אוֹמֵר: מִנַּיִן אַתָּה אוֹמֵר שֶׁלָּקוּ הַמִּצְרִים בְּמִצְרַיִם עֶשֶׂר מַכּוֹת וְעַל הַיָּם לָקוּ חֲמִשִּׁים מַכּוֹת,

בְּמִצְרַיִם מָה הוּא אוֹמֵר: וַיֹּאמְרוּ הַחַרְטֻמִּם אֶל פַּרְעֹה אֶצְבַּע אֱלֹהִים הִיא:

וְעַל הַיָּם מָה הוּא אוֹמֵר: וַיַּרְא יִשְׂרָאֵל אֶת הַיָּד הַגְּדֹלָה אֲשֶׁר עָשָׂה יְיָ בְּמִצְרַיִם, וַיִּירְאוּ הָעָם אֶת יְיָ, וַיַּאֲמִינוּ בַּיְיָ וּבְמֹשֶׁה עַבְדּוֹ: כַּמָּה לָקוּ בְּאֶצְבַּע, עֶשֶׂר מַכּוֹת, אֱמוֹר מֵעַתָּה:

בְּמִצְרַיִם לָקוּ עֶשֶׂר מַכּוֹת, וְעַל הַיָּם לָקוּ חֲמִשִּׁים מַכּוֹת:

Someone else out loud:

RABBI Eliezer took this calculation a step further.

How do we know that each individual plague which God brought upon the Egyptians in Egypt consisted of four plagues?

Well, I'll tell you:

Here's how the Psalms describes the plagues: *"He sent against them His fierce anger, fury, wrath, and torment, a dispatch of nasty angels."*

Fury is one.

Wrath makes two.

Torment makes three.

Dispatch of nasty angels makes four.

4 x 10 = 40. So it turns out that in Egypt they were struck by forty plagues.

40 x 5 = 200. So at the sea they were struck by two hundred plagues.

רַבִּי אֱלִיעֶזֶר אוֹמֵר: מִנַּיִן שֶׁכָּל מַכָּה וּמַכָּה שֶׁהֵבִיא הַקָּדוֹשׁ בָּרוּךְ הוּא עַל הַמִּצְרִים בְּמִצְרַיִם הָיְתָה שֶׁל אַרְבַּע מַכּוֹת,

שֶׁנֶּאֱמַר: יְשַׁלַּח בָּם חֲרוֹן אַפּוֹ, עֶבְרָה, וָזַעַם, וְצָרָה, מִשְׁלַחַת מַלְאֲכֵי רָעִים:

עֶבְרָה אַחַת, וָזַעַם שְׁתַּיִם, וְצָרָה שָׁלֹשׁ, מִשְׁלַחַת מַלְאֲכֵי רָעִים אַרְבַּע, אֱמוֹר מֵעַתָּה: בְּמִצְרַיִם לָקוּ אַרְבָּעִים מַכּוֹת, וְעַל הַיָּם לָקוּ מָאתַיִם מַכּוֹת:

Everyone:

רַבִּי יְהוּדָה הָיָה נוֹתֵן בָּהֶם סִמָּנִים:

RABBI Yehudah gave us a way to remember these ten plagues in order, by combining the first letter of each, forming three words:

Pour out a drop of wine as you say each of these, with the same thoughts as above.

 Everyone:

דְּצַ"ךְ Blood, Frogs, Lice **(Deh-tzahkh)**

עֲדַ"שׁ Wild Beasts, Livestock Disease, Boils **(Ah-dahsh)**

בְּאַחַ"ב Hail, Locusts, Darkness, Firstborn **(Beh-ah-khav)**

Once you're done, remove that dish with the wine you spilled and dispose of that wine. Now refill your cups all the way.

Counting the Plagues

 Someone out loud:

Remember the five rabbis who were sitting around the entire night, telling the Passover story? Here's another instance where three of those rabbis were discussing Exodus stuff:

 IT SEEMS these rabbis understood the plagues as a sort of detox program for Egypt. People's behavior, words and thoughts leave negative energy in the environment. The plagues of blood, frogs, etc., were the effects of that negativity being released. That bad energy wasn't letting us leave. But once it was cleaned up, we could get released too.

All matter is composed of four qualities that the ancients called fire, wind, water and earth. We would probably call them positive, negative, matter and antimatter.[38] And then there's the quintessence of everything, the very fabric of existence.

If the human being is capable only of affecting the outer layer of reality, then each plague was one detox. But if we affect the basic elements of reality, then a quadruple detox was needed. And if human behavior affects the core substance of reality, then each plague had to be a five-step program.[39]

The BIG Traditional Wine-Spilling Ceremony

Hold on. You're about to spill from your cup thirteen more times—once as you mention each plague, and then three more. Have in mind just the same as we had above.

By the time we're done, you'll have poured a total of sixteen spills. At that point, the wine remaining will have become "wine that makes joy"—so you won't spill out any more. Instead, you'll add more wine to the cup at that point, so that it will be full.

 Pour a drop of wine from your cup into a broken dish as you say each of the ten plagues (ten spills in all):

דָם Blood (Dahm)

צְפַרְדֵעַ Frogs (Tze-fahr-day-ah)

כִּנִּים Lice (Kee-neem)

עָרוֹב Wild Beasts (Ah-rohv)

דֶבֶר Livestock Disease (Deh-vehr)

שְׁחִין Boils (Sheh-kheen)

בָּרָד Hail (Bah-rahd)

אַרְבֶּה Locusts (Ahr-beh)

חֹשֶׁךְ Darkness (Khoh-shehkh)

מַכַּת בְּכוֹרוֹת Slaying of the Firstborn (Mah-kaht beh-khoh-roht.)

56

Someone out loud:

דָּבָר אַחֵר: בְּיָד חֲזָקָה שְׁתַּיִם, וּבִזְרֹעַ נְטוּיָה שְׁתַּיִם, וּבְמֹרָא גָּדֹל שְׁתַּיִם, וּבְאֹתוֹת שְׁתַּיִם, וּבְמֹפְתִים שְׁתַּיִם:

ALL that was one unpacking of "a strong hand and with an outstretched arm, with a huge display, with signs, and with wonders." Now for another one:

A strong hand—just "hand" would be one plague, but "strong hand" must be two.

An outstretched arm—another two plagues: arm + outstretched.

A huge display—two more: huge + display.

Signs—plural, so two more.

Wonders—also plural, so another two.

2 x 5 = 10.

אֵלּוּ עֶשֶׂר מַכּוֹת שֶׁהֵבִיא הַקָּדוֹשׁ בָּרוּךְ הוּא עַל הַמִּצְרִים בְּמִצְרַיִם, וְאֵלּוּ הֵן:

THOSE are the Ten Plagues that the Holy One, blessed be He, brought upon the Egyptians, namely...

The Traditional Wine-Spilling Ceremony

Here's what's going to happen right now: You're about to complete this verse, with its reference to blood and other stuff. But as you do it, you and everyone else at the table are going to pour out a few drops of wine for every mention of a plague.

This wine-spilling ceremony is very precise. You hold your cup of wine in your right hand. You pour just a little wine, one tiny spill as you say each word, into a broken bowl. You don't want to drink wine that's associated with plagues, so it's important that you have in mind that you're not saying them over the wine in the cup, but on the wine that you're pouring out of the cup—which you'll dispose of later.

NOW HERE'S THE KABBALISTIC INSTRUCTIONS: The cup is acting as what the Kabbalists refer to as *Malchut*. That's the last and ultimate of the ten modalities by which God creates and directs the world.

You're pouring wine that's acting as what Kabbalists refer to as "anger and wrath" out of that cup.

You're doing this with the power of Understanding. That's the second of the Ten Divine Modalities.

You're pouring it into a broken container, which is the secret of *kelipah*, which is called "cursed." *Kelipah* means a shell, or a husk. It's the way God's light is obstructed, so that things appear separate from Him. That's how evil emerges.

Wine that remains in the cup once we're done is called "wine that brings happiness."

If we pour out wine because we're concerned that they absorbed bad energy from mention of the plagues, how much more careful we should be to speak only good things when we eat and drink the whole year long. It's important not only that you consume good food, but that you also consume it in a good way, thinking and saying the right things, so that you'll get the right energy out of your food.[37]

Pour a drop of wine from your cup into a broken dish as you say each of the following three phrases:

דָּם   blood **(Dahm)**

וָאֵשׁ   and fire **(Vah-aysh)**

וְתִימְרוֹת עָשָׁן: and pillars of smoke as tall as date palms. **(Veh-tim-roht ah-shahn)**

...and with signs... וּבְאֹתוֹת, זֶה הַמַּטֶּה, כְּמָה שֶׁנֶּאֱמַר: וְאֶת הַמַּטֶּה הַזֶּה תִּקַּח בְּיָדֶךָ, אֲשֶׁר תַּעֲשֶׂה בּוֹ אֶת הָאֹתֹת:

That's talking about Moses' staff.

God told Moses that when Pharaoh would ask for a sign that it really was God sending him, he should throw down his staff and it would turn into a snake.

When Pharaoh's research team pulled off a simulation of that exercise, Moses' staff-snake reverted to stick-snake status—and then devoured the Egyptian specimens. That was a sign that Moses really was representing the Creator of heaven and earth.

In fact, God explicitly made this connection when He first told Moses to take the staff with Him. He said:

"Take this staff in your hand. You're going to do *signs* with it."

...and with wonders... וּבְמֹפְתִים, זֶה הַדָּם, כְּמָה שֶׁנֶּאֱמַר: וְנָתַתִּי מוֹפְתִים בַּשָּׁמַיִם וּבָאָרֶץ—

That refers to the miracle of turning the waters of the Nile into blood. There's a verse that makes that connection:

"I will show *wonders* in heaven and on earth...

And the next word is "blood." But just hold on to that, because we're about to do...

...with a strong hand...

בְּיָד חֲזָקָה, זֶה הַדֶּבֶר, כְּמָה שֶׁנֶּאֱמַר: הִנֵּה יַד יְיָ הוֹיָה בְּמִקְנְךָ אֲשֶׁר בַּשָּׂדֶה, בַּסּוּסִים בַּחֲמֹרִים בַּגְּמַלִּים בַּבָּקָר וּבַצֹּאן, דֶּבֶר כָּבֵד מְאֹד:

That's talking about the disease that struck the Egyptian livestock:

"And now, the hand of God will be on your livestock in the field—on the horses, the donkeys, the camels, the herds and the flocks. It will be a very severe disease."

...with an outstretched arm...

וּבִזְרֹעַ נְטוּיָה, זוֹ הַחֶרֶב, כְּמָה שֶׁנֶּאֱמַר: וְחַרְבּוֹ שְׁלוּפָה בְּיָדוֹ נְטוּיָה עַל יְרוּשָׁלָיִם:

That's referring to the heavenly sword that struck the firstborn Egyptians. How do we know? Because "stretching out" is used when talking about swords,[36] as in:

"His sword was drawn in his hand, *stretched out* over Jerusalem."

...with a huge display

וּבְמֹרָא גָּדֹל, זֶה גִּלּוּי שְׁכִינָה, כְּמָה שֶׁנֶּאֱמַר: אוֹ הֲנִסָּה אֱלֹהִים לָבוֹא לָקַחַת לוֹ גוֹי מִקֶּרֶב גּוֹי בְּמַסֹּת בְּאֹתֹת וּבְמוֹפְתִים וּבְמִלְחָמָה וּבְיָד חֲזָקָה וּבִזְרוֹעַ נְטוּיָה וּבְמוֹרָאִים גְּדֹלִים, כְּכֹל אֲשֶׁר עָשָׂה לָכֶם יְיָ אֱלֹהֵיכֶם בְּמִצְרַיִם לְעֵינֶיךָ:

That's talking about the open display of God's presence (a.k.a. "the Shechinah"). Moses later pointed this out to the people, when he (rhetorically) asked:

"Has any god ever tried to extract a nation for himself out of another nation? And do it with proofs, signs and wonders, with war and with a strong hand and an outstretched arm, and with huge displays? Well, that's what God your God did for you in Egypt right before your very eyes."

 HEY, that's a good point, isn't it? Why does no one else have a story about their people being miraculously liberated and entering into a covenant with God? It seems it never occurred anywhere else. And it's not something you can make up and pass off as national history—otherwise, for sure some other people would have come up with the same idea.

> **WAIT A MINUTE!** What's this "And God knew" business? Doesn't God always know? Isn't that part of His job description as Omniscient God?
>
> But knowing, in Hebrew, means a lot more than awareness. It means engaging yourself with something. As in "Adam knew Eve." You really know something only when you engage yourself with it.
>
> So, yes, God is aware of everything happening in His world. The world happens only because He's aware of it happening. But the point here is that bad stuff was happening that got the Creator of the Universe re-engaged with His universe. And that re-engagement brought about miracles and liberation.[35]

Unpacking a Packed Passage, Part 4

Someone else out loud:

וַיּוֹצִיאֵנוּ יְיָ מִמִּצְרַיִם בְּיָד חֲזָקָה וּבִזְרֹעַ נְטוּיָה וּבְמֹרָא גָדֹל וּבְאֹתוֹת וּבְמֹפְתִים:

AND God took us out of Egypt with a strong hand and with an outstretched arm, with a huge display, with signs, and with wonders.

Now let's unpack that:

וַיּוֹצִיאֵנוּ יְיָ מִמִּצְרַיִם, לֹא עַל יְדֵי מַלְאָךְ וְלֹא עַל יְדֵי שָׂרָף וְלֹא עַל יְדֵי שָׁלִיחַ, אֶלָּא הַקָּדוֹשׁ בָּרוּךְ הוּא בִּכְבוֹדוֹ וּבְעַצְמוֹ, שֶׁנֶּאֱמַר:

God took us out of Egypt...

He didn't send an angel to do the job for Him, or a seraph, or a messenger. The same God who is beyond everything in this world took care of it Himself! That's also how it's told in the original story:

וְעָבַרְתִּי בְאֶרֶץ מִצְרַיִם בַּלַּיְלָה הַזֶּה, וְהִכֵּיתִי כָל בְּכוֹר בְּאֶרֶץ מִצְרַיִם מֵאָדָם וְעַד בְּהֵמָה, וּבְכָל אֱלֹהֵי מִצְרַיִם אֶעֱשֶׂה שְׁפָטִים, אֲנִי יְיָ:

"On that night I will pass through the land of Egypt. I will strike every firstborn in the land of Egypt, from man to beast. And I will carry out judgments against all the gods of Egypt, I, God."

וְעָבַרְתִּי בְאֶרֶץ מִצְרַיִם, אֲנִי וְלֹא מַלְאָךְ. וְהִכֵּיתִי כָל בְּכוֹר בְּאֶרֶץ מִצְרַיִם, אֲנִי וְלֹא שָׂרָף. וּבְכָל אֱלֹהֵי מִצְרַיִם אֶעֱשֶׂה שְׁפָטִים, אֲנִי וְלֹא הַשָּׁלִיחַ. אֲנִי יְיָ, אֲנִי הוּא וְלֹא אַחֵר:

"I will pass through the land of Egypt"—I Myself, and not an angel.

"And I will strike every firstborn in the land of Egypt"—I Myself, and not a seraph.

"And I will carry out judgments against all the gods of Egypt"—I Myself, and not a messenger.

"I, God"—I Myself, and none other.

Unpacking a Packed Passage, Part 3

Someone else out loud:

וַנִּצְעַק אֶל יְיָ אֱלֹהֵי אֲבֹתֵינוּ, וַיִּשְׁמַע יְיָ אֶת קֹלֵנוּ, וַיַּרְא אֶת עָנְיֵנוּ וְאֶת עֲמָלֵנוּ וְאֶת לַחֲצֵנוּ:

AND we cried out to God, the God of our fathers, and God heard our voice and saw our suffering, our labor and our oppression.

Now to unpack that:

And we cried out to God, the God of our fathers...

וַנִּצְעַק אֶל יְיָ אֱלֹהֵי אֲבֹתֵינוּ, כְּמָה שֶׁנֶּאֱמַר: וַיְהִי בַיָּמִים הָרַבִּים הָהֵם וַיָּמָת מֶלֶךְ מִצְרַיִם, וַיֵּאָנְחוּ בְנֵי יִשְׂרָאֵל מִן הָעֲבֹדָה וַיִּזְעָקוּ, וַתַּעַל שַׁוְעָתָם אֶל הָאֱלֹהִים מִן הָעֲבֹדָה:

That's how the story in Exodus continues:

"It was during that long period of time that the king of Egypt died. The Children of Israel groaned from their labor. They cried out, and their cry to be saved from their work rose up to God."

...and God heard our voice...

וַיִּשְׁמַע יְיָ אֶת קֹלֵנוּ, כְּמָה שֶׁנֶּאֱמַר: וַיִּשְׁמַע אֱלֹהִים אֶת נַאֲקָתָם, וַיִּזְכֹּר אֱלֹהִים אֶת בְּרִיתוֹ אֶת אַבְרָהָם אֶת יִצְחָק וְאֶת יַעֲקֹב:

That's the next part of the story:

"God heard their groans, and God remembered His covenant that He had made with Abraham, with Isaac and with Jacob."

...and saw our suffering...

וַיַּרְא אֶת עָנְיֵנוּ, זוֹ פְּרִישׁוּת דֶּרֶךְ אֶרֶץ, כְּמָה שֶׁנֶּאֱמַר: וַיַּרְא אֱלֹהִים אֶת בְּנֵי יִשְׂרָאֵל, וַיֵּדַע אֱלֹהִים:

That's referring to how the Egyptians disrupted marital relations. That's also hinted to in Exodus:

"And God saw the Children of Israel. And God knew."

...our labor...

וְאֶת עֲמָלֵנוּ, אֵלּוּ הַבָּנִים, כְּמָה שֶׁנֶּאֱמַר: כָּל הַבֵּן הַיִּלּוֹד הַיְאֹרָה תַּשְׁלִיכֻהוּ, וְכָל הַבַּת תְּחַיּוּן:

That's referring to what Pharaoh told the Egyptians to do to the children:

"Every boy that is born, you shall throw into the river, and every girl you shall keep alive."

...and our oppression.

וְאֶת לַחֲצֵנוּ, זֶה הַדְּחַק, כְּמָה שֶׁנֶּאֱמַר: וְגַם רָאִיתִי אֶת הַלַּחַץ אֲשֶׁר מִצְרַיִם לֹחֲצִים אֹתָם:

That's talking about the extreme pressure we were under, as God noted to Moses:

"I have seen the oppression with which the Egyptians oppress them."

וַיְעַנּוּנוּ, כְּמָה שֶׁנֶּאֱמַר: וַיָּשִׂימוּ עָלָיו שָׂרֵי מִסִּים לְמַעַן עַנֹּתוֹ בְּסִבְלֹתָם, וַיִּבֶן עָרֵי מִסְכְּנוֹת לְפַרְעֹה, אֶת פִּתֹם וְאֶת רַעַמְסֵס:

...and they made us suffer...

That's a reference to the next part of the story:

"They set taskmasters over the Jews to make them suffer under their load. The Jews built storage cities for Pharaoh, namely Pitom and Ramses."

וַיִּתְּנוּ עָלֵינוּ עֲבֹדָה קָשָׁה, כְּמָה שֶׁנֶּאֱמַר: וַיַּעֲבִדוּ מִצְרַיִם אֶת בְּנֵי יִשְׂרָאֵל בְּפָרֶךְ: וַיְמָרְרוּ אֶת חַיֵּיהֶם בַּעֲבֹדָה קָשָׁה בְּחֹמֶר וּבִלְבֵנִים וּבְכָל עֲבֹדָה בַּשָּׂדֶה, אֵת כָּל עֲבֹדָתָם אֲשֶׁר עָבְדוּ בָהֶם בְּפָרֶךְ:

...and they assigned us hard work.

That's the next part of the story:

"The Egyptians made the Children of Israel work under body-and-soul-breaking conditions. They embittered their lives with hard work, with mortar and with bricks and all kinds of field work. Everything they made them do was to break them."

IF YOU'RE IDENTIFYING with this story, that may be because it sums up the human condition. We're all slaves of Pharaoh. We're enslaved by our positions in life, by our everyday tasks, and just by having physical bodies. That's our Egypt.

We feel that way because we don't really belong where we are. Because we're all God's children, divine sparks sent to earth on a mission to heal and transform the world, to build a home for God on a Godly planet. But we can't do that if we stay trapped where we are, stressed out about building yet bigger and yet more impressive monuments for our own Pharaohs.

A plant that is not allowed to grow is imprisoned. The same with an animal that's not allowed to move. Or a human being not allowed to think. And so too, a soul not allowed to do all its mitzvahs.[33]

We need to escape our personal limitations, to break the chains that don't let us complete our divine mission. And that's our Exodus.

There's a key difference, however. In Egypt, we could only wait for God to take us out from there with miracles and wonders. In our case, God is also waiting for us to do some miracles and wonders.

That's why He gave us the Torah, to show us how to make miracles. To take the mud of a mundane world and transform it into the building bricks of a beautiful world.

We do our miracle, and He will do the rest.[34]

THE HAGGADAH doesn't unpack these metaphors, but here's the traditional meaning:

In Egypt, we were downtrodden and beaten till we bled. But God gave us two blood-mitzvahs so that we would be worthy of liberation: The blood of the Passover lamb that we painted on our doorposts, and the blood of circumcision (since all males had to circumcise before leaving).

The oppression of Egypt that was meant to destroy us actually made us greater, more powerful, more mature and much more beautiful in God's eyes. The women were determined to continue having children, and so they prettied themselves up and brought food to eat with their husbands out in the field. This way, they ensured the continuity of the Jewish people.

But we were still naked and bare. Mitzvahs are clothing for the soul. We had to get to Sinai to get that clothing.[31]

Unpacking a Packed Passage, Part 2

 *Someone else out loud:*

וַיָּרֵעוּ אֹתָנוּ הַמִּצְרִים וַיְעַנּוּנוּ, וַיִּתְּנוּ עָלֵינוּ עֲבֹדָה קָשָׁה:

Now let's take a look at the next verse we would say there in the Temple:

THE Egyptians treated us badly and they made us suffer, and they assigned us hard work.

Unpacking that now:

The Egyptians treated us badly...

That's a reference to the story in Exodus, where Pharaoh says to his people:

"Come, let us act cunningly with these people. Otherwise they'll keep multiplying, and then, what if there's a war against us? They will join our enemies, fight against us, and go up out of the land!"

וַיָּרֵעוּ אֹתָנוּ הַמִּצְרִים, כְּמָה שֶׁנֶּאֱמַר: הָבָה נִתְחַכְּמָה לוֹ, פֶּן יִרְבֶּה, וְהָיָה כִּי תִקְרֶאנָה מִלְחָמָה, וְנוֹסַף גַּם הוּא עַל שֹׂנְאֵינוּ, וְנִלְחַם בָּנוּ וְעָלָה מִן הָאָרֶץ:

 THE LITERAL translation is "The Egyptians made us bad." Meaning, they infected us with their own badness. That's why we had to be yanked out of there fast and earlier than predicted. Which meant that the entire crucible-for-our-souls effect that Egyptian slavery was meant to accomplish was incomplete. And that meant we had to finish off that process in later exiles.[32]

בִּמְתֵי מְעָט, כְּמָה שֶׁנֶּאֱמַר: בְּשִׁבְעִים נֶפֶשׁ יָרְדוּ אֲבֹתֶיךָ מִצְרָיְמָה, וְעַתָּה שָׂמְךָ יְיָ אֱלֹהֶיךָ כְּכוֹכְבֵי הַשָּׁמַיִם לָרֹב:

...with very few people...

That's just like Moses said:

"There were only seventy people when your fathers descended to Egypt. But now, God your God has made you as plentiful as the stars of the heavens."

וַיְהִי שָׁם לְגוֹי, מְלַמֵּד שֶׁהָיוּ יִשְׂרָאֵל מְצֻיָּנִים שָׁם:

...but he ended up being a people...

That tells us that the Jewish People stood out there. They were a distinct people, a people apart.

גָּדוֹל עָצוּם, כְּמָה שֶׁנֶּאֱמַר: וּבְנֵי יִשְׂרָאֵל פָּרוּ וַיִּשְׁרְצוּ וַיִּרְבּוּ וַיַּעַצְמוּ בִּמְאֹד מְאֹד וַתִּמָּלֵא הָאָרֶץ אֹתָם:

...a mighty people, powerful...

That's a reference to what the Exodus story tells:

"And the Children of Israel were fruitful and swarmed and increased and became very, very powerful. The land was filled with them."

וָרָב, כְּמָה שֶׁנֶּאֱמַר: וָאֶעֱבֹר עָלַיִךְ וָאֶרְאֵךְ מִתְבּוֹסֶסֶת בְּדָמָיִךְ, וָאֹמַר לָךְ בְּדָמַיִךְ חֲיִי, וָאֹמַר לָךְ בְּדָמַיִךְ חֲיִי: רְבָבָה כְּצֶמַח הַשָּׂדֶה נְתַתִּיךְ, וַתִּרְבִּי וַתִּגְדְּלִי וַתָּבֹאִי בַּעֲדִי עֲדָיִים, שָׁדַיִם נָכֹנוּ וּשְׂעָרֵךְ צִמֵּחַ, וְאַתְּ עֵרֹם וְעֶרְיָה:

...and populous.

Like the prophet Ezekiel described the Jewish People when God saved them from Egypt (using powerful metaphors that cry out for unpacking):

"And I passed over you and I saw you wallowing in your blood.

So I said to you, 'In your blood shall you live.' And I said to you, 'In your blood shall you live.' I made you thrive like the plants of the field, and you grew and you matured and you became very beautiful, your bosom well-formed and your hair grown long. But you were naked and bare."

Unpacking a Packed Passage, Part 1

 NOW we'll start telling the story of our descent to Egypt, our enslavement, and our liberation from there. We'll do that by taking four terse lines of Torah that pack in the entire story, unpacking them one by one for the details that appear elsewhere in Torah or the Prophets. As we do that, everybody should add in more details that they've learned, or implications that they see in there.

The verses we'll use are those we would say when we brought our first fruits to the Temple. We gave a basket of produce to a Kohen and recited these verses to tell the story of the Exodus and to thank God for the Promised Land. Since everyone knew them by heart, they served as the everyman's Jewish history in a nutshell. So they're packed tight with meaning.[30]

To make things clearer, here's the entire passage that we're going to unpack:

1. An Aramean was out to annihilate my father. Eventually, he went down to Egypt. He was just visiting, bringing only a few people, but ended up becoming a mighty people there, powerful and populous. (Deut. 26:5)

2. The Egyptians treated us badly and they made us suffer, and they assigned us hard work. (Deut. 26:6)

3. And we cried out to God, the God of our fathers, and God heard our voice and saw our suffering, our labor and our oppression. (Deut. 26:7)

4. And God took us out of Egypt with a strong hand and with an outstretched arm, with a huge display, with signs and with wonders. (Deut. 26:8)

 *Someone out loud:*

וַיֵּרֶד מִצְרַיְמָה, אָנוּס עַל פִּי הַדִּבּוּר:

Let's unpack the verse we just quoted:

He went down to Egypt.

That's telling us that Jacob went down to Egypt by divine decree. He had no choice. It was decided beforehand that this had to happen.

He was just visiting there...

וַיָּגָר שָׁם, מְלַמֵּד שֶׁלֹּא יָרַד יַעֲקֹב אָבִינוּ לְהִשְׁתַּקֵּעַ בְּמִצְרַיִם אֶלָּא לָגוּר שָׁם, שֶׁנֶּאֱמַר: וַיֹּאמְרוּ אֶל פַּרְעֹה לָגוּר בָּאָרֶץ בָּאנוּ, כִּי אֵין מִרְעֶה לַצֹּאן אֲשֶׁר לַעֲבָדֶיךָ, כִּי כָבֵד הָרָעָב בְּאֶרֶץ כְּנָעַן, וְעַתָּה יֵשְׁבוּ נָא עֲבָדֶיךָ בְּאֶרֶץ גֹּשֶׁן:

That means Jacob never went there to stay, just for a short visit. Take a look at what his sons said to Pharaoh:

"We've just come for a short stay in the land. You see, there's no pasture left for us in Canaan because the famine is so bad there. So now could you please let your servants [i.e., Jacob & sons] sit it out for a while in the Goshen territory?"

**Veh-hee sheh-ahm-dah lah-ah-voh-tay-noo veh-lah-noo
Sheh-loh eh-khahd bil-vahd ah-mahd ah-lay-noo leh-kha-loh-tay-noo
Eh-lah sheh-beh-khohl dohr vah-dohr ohm-deem ah-lay-noo leh-kha-loh-tay-noo
Veh-hah-kah-dohsh bah-rookh hoo mah-tzee-lay-noo mee-yah-dahm.**

 Put down the cup and uncover the matzah again.

PEOPLE ARE LOOKING for miracles. Why did they happen back then and not today?

But if you know a little history, you'll realize that the fact that you are here today and you know you are a Jew is the greatest of miracles and the strongest evidence of our covenant with God.[27] Just because we don't notice the miracles doesn't make them any less miraculous.

Divine Protection at Work

 Someone out loud:

צֵא וּלְמַד מַה בִּקֵּשׁ לָבָן הָאֲרַמִּי לַעֲשׂוֹת לְיַעֲקֹב אָבִינוּ, שֶׁפַּרְעֹה לֹא גָזַר אֶלָּא עַל הַזְּכָרִים, וְלָבָן בִּקֵּשׁ לַעֲקוֹר אֶת הַכֹּל,

Let's step out of the Exodus story for a minute to see God's protection at work with the prototype Jew, Jacob. Then we'll see how the same thing unfolds in Egypt.

TAKE a look at what Laban the Aramean attempted to do to Jacob, father of all us Jews. After all, Pharaoh only made a decree against baby boys, but Laban was out to uproot the entire nation.

That was when Jacob picked up his entire family to get out of the clutches of Laban, his corrupt father-in-law.

Laban got wind of this and chased after him. But God intervened, appearing to Laban in a dream, warning him not to hurt Jacob.[28]

שֶׁנֶּאֱמַר: אֲרַמִּי אֹבֵד אָבִי, וַיֵּרֶד מִצְרַיְמָה וַיָּגָר שָׁם בִּמְתֵי מְעָט, וַיְהִי שָׁם לְגוֹי גָּדוֹל עָצוּם וָרָב:

Like it says:

An Aramean was out to annihilate my father. Eventually, he went down to Egypt. He was just visiting there with very few people, but he ended up becoming a mighty people there, powerful and populous.[29]

ABRAHAM was the first iconoclast—meaning, literally, an idol-smasher.

Abraham saw that demagogues were abusing the natural awe and wonder of the human soul to establish their power over society. All on his own, he rediscovered a forgotten truth—that there's really only one source of all power and existence, and He has nothing to do with what these charlatans were preaching.

Most importantly, Abraham had a conviction that this All-Powerful Being is just, and cares about what's going on down here with us little creatures. And so, he stood up for justice and compassion.

And that's how the Jewish People got started.[26]

The Promise of Protection

Someone out loud:

בָּרוּךְ שׁוֹמֵר הַבְטָחָתוֹ לְיִשְׂרָאֵל, בָּרוּךְ הוּא, שֶׁהַקָּדוֹשׁ בָּרוּךְ הוּא חִשַּׁב אֶת הַקֵּץ לַעֲשׂוֹת כְּמָה שֶׁאָמַר לְאַבְרָהָם אָבִינוּ בִּבְרִית בֵּין הַבְּתָרִים, שֶׁנֶּאֱמַר: וַיֹּאמֶר לְאַבְרָם: יָדֹעַ תֵּדַע כִּי גֵר יִהְיֶה זַרְעֲךָ בְּאֶרֶץ לֹא לָהֶם, וַעֲבָדוּם וְעִנּוּ אֹתָם, אַרְבַּע מֵאוֹת שָׁנָה: וְגַם אֶת הַגּוֹי אֲשֶׁר יַעֲבֹדוּ דָּן אָנֹכִי, וְאַחֲרֵי כֵן יֵצְאוּ בִּרְכֻשׁ גָּדוֹל:

"**BLESSED** is the One who keeps His promise to Israel, blessed be He!

You see, the Holy One Blessed Be He cut down our exile by calculating 400 years from the birth of Isaac.

Here's what He said to our father Abraham in the Covenant Between the Parts:

"Know that your children are going to be strangers in a land that does not belong to them for four hundred years. They are going to be enslaved and oppressed. Also know that I won't let off the hook the nation that enslaves them. And after that, they'll get out of there with a lot of wealth."

 Now cover the matzah, lift up your cups, and chant:

Everyone:

וְהִיא שֶׁעָמְדָה לַאֲבוֹתֵינוּ וְלָנוּ, שֶׁלֹּא אֶחָד בִּלְבַד עָמַד עָלֵינוּ לְכַלּוֹתֵנוּ אֶלָּא שֶׁבְּכָל דּוֹר וָדוֹר עוֹמְדִים עָלֵינוּ לְכַלּוֹתֵנוּ, וְהַקָּדוֹשׁ בָּרוּךְ הוּא מַצִּילֵנוּ מִיָּדָם:

IT'S this promise that has stood for our ancestors and for us.

Because not just one nation alone has arisen against us to wipe us out. In every generation, there are those who stand against us to wipe us out.

And each time, the Holy One, blessed be He, saves us from their hand.

YOU MAY HAVE HEARD of the fifth child.

That's the one who didn't turn up tonight. Probably not his fault. He might not even know it's Passover. If he would, and if he knew how much we would like to see him, good chance he would be real eager to come.

This Seder is for the fifth child as well. Because if we're inspired enough by this Seder, we'll make sure that fifth child will be at the next one.[25]

The Answer: Take Two

AS WITH MOST THINGS JEWISH, there's more than one opinion on how to tell the story of the Exodus.

Everyone agrees that we start with what was wrong and end with what went right. One opinion is that what was wrong was that we were slaves in Egypt. The other opinion is that it started long before that, when we were idolaters.

In Torah, two opinions can both be true, so we have two beginnings of the story.

Someone out loud:

מִתְּחִלָּה עוֹבְדֵי עֲבוֹדָה זָרָה הָיוּ אֲבוֹתֵינוּ, וְעַכְשָׁו קֵרְבָנוּ הַמָּקוֹם לַעֲבֹדָתוֹ, שֶׁנֶּאֱמַר: וַיֹּאמֶר יְהוֹשֻׁעַ אֶל כָּל הָעָם, כֹּה אָמַר יְיָ אֱלֹהֵי יִשְׂרָאֵל: בְּעֵבֶר הַנָּהָר יָשְׁבוּ אֲבוֹתֵיכֶם מֵעוֹלָם, תֶּרַח אֲבִי אַבְרָהָם וַאֲבִי נָחוֹר, וַיַּעַבְדוּ אֱלֹהִים אֲחֵרִים:

Now, here's an embarrassing and shameful fact, that we're going to have to admit:

ORIGINALLY, our ancestors were idolaters. But now, the One Who Encompasses Everything has brought us into a great deal, working exclusively for Him.

That's what Joshua said to all the people:

So says God, the God of Israel, "Your fathers lived on the other side of the river for a long time. There was Terach, the father of Abraham and Nahor. And they served other gods.

וָאֶקַּח אֶת אֲבִיכֶם אֶת אַבְרָהָם מֵעֵבֶר הַנָּהָר, וָאוֹלֵךְ אוֹתוֹ בְּכָל אֶרֶץ כְּנָעַן, וָאַרְבֶּה אֶת זַרְעוֹ וָאֶתֵּן לוֹ אֶת יִצְחָק: וָאֶתֵּן לְיִצְחָק אֶת יַעֲקֹב וְאֶת עֵשָׂו, וָאֶתֵּן לְעֵשָׂו אֶת הַר שֵׂעִיר לָרֶשֶׁת אוֹתוֹ, וְיַעֲקֹב וּבָנָיו יָרְדוּ מִצְרָיִם:

"**SO** I took your father Abraham from the other side of the river and I walked him through the whole land of Canaan. I gave him lots of descendants. I gave him Isaac. To Isaac I gave Jacob and Esau. To Esau, I gave Mount Seir to take over. Jacob and his children went down to Egypt."

IF YOU'RE NOT inquisitively challenged, you're probably asking: Where does the Torah speak about four children?

Well, it speaks about them by bringing up their questions. For three of them, that is. In one of the four instances of parent-to-child transmission of this story, the question is absent. That's child #4—the child that doesn't ask.

Perhaps that's because he's kind of absent himself. Sure, he's sitting there at the Seder. He goes through all the motions. He does exactly what he's supposed to do. But if he were really there, in mind, heart and soul, he would have questions.

Your job then is to open him up, get him engaged. Get him to ask questions. Otherwise, how will he learn?[23]

The Question of the Inquisitively Challenged Child[24]

 Someone else out loud:

יָכוֹל מֵרֹאשׁ חֹדֶשׁ, תַּלְמוּד לוֹמַר: בַּיּוֹם הַהוּא. אִי בַּיּוֹם הַהוּא, יָכוֹל מִבְּעוֹד יוֹם, תַּלְמוּד לוֹמַר: בַּעֲבוּר זֶה, בַּעֲבוּר זֶה לֹא אָמַרְתִּי אֶלָּא בְּשָׁעָה שֶׁיֵּשׁ מַצָּה וּמָרוֹר מֻנָּחִים לְפָנֶיךָ:

Two Voices:

You: **Hold on, maybe we were supposed to do this Seder on Rosh Chodesh—15 days ago, on the first day of the month!**

Kid: Umm. Why then?

You: **Because that's when God told Moses about the mitzvah of Passover.**

Kid: Okay, so we messed up.

You: **Nope, it says on *that* day.**

Kid: Okay, so let's get on. What do we say next?

You: **Not so simple. Because then we should be doing it during the day. Now it's night already.**

Kid: So it's over. Let's eat.

You: **Not so fast. You see, it says "for the sake of this stuff." Meaning this matzah and bitter herbs that we eat on the night of Passover. So we have to wait until we're supposed to eat that stuff—and that's tonight.**

Kid: But why do we have to tell a story to food?

 Someone out loud:

See? It worked!

OF COURSE, this time around, he'll come with us. Only if he had been there, before the Torah was given, would he never have been liberated.

But now that the Torah has made us into an indivisible whole, nobody will be left behind. Whether you're inspired or not, practicing or rebelling, you remain an irreplaceable part of the Jewish People.

And maybe when he hears that, he'll get how amazing this Torah is—that it connects us together no matter what. Maybe that's why we put him next to the bright child—so that he can teach him how precious and valuable he is to his people.[21]

The Simple One

 Someone else out loud:

תָּם מַה הוּא אוֹמֵר: מַה זֹּאת,
וְאָמַרְתָּ אֵלָיו: בְּחֹזֶק יָד
הוֹצִיאָנוּ יְיָ מִמִּצְרַיִם מִבֵּית עֲבָדִים:

WHAT about the simple one? Well, he just sits there in total amazement and says, "What is this?" So you tell him about all the amazing miracles, saying, "With a mighty hand, God took us out of Egypt, where we were slaves!"

 THE SIMPLE CHILD may not be too bright, but in a way, he's more in touch with God.

First of all, because God is simple. When you're complicated, you end up going in circles and you lose the simple point at the center, a.k.a. God. That's something bright people need to learn from simple people.[22]

Secondly, because he's forever in wonder. As soon as you've lost wonder, you've lost touch with truth.

Which brings us to the next child...

The Inquisitively Challenged One

 *Someone else out loud:*

 וְשֶׁאֵינוֹ יוֹדֵעַ לִשְׁאוֹל,
אַתְּ פְּתַח לוֹ,
שֶׁנֶּאֱמַר: וְהִגַּדְתָּ לְבִנְךָ בַּיּוֹם הַהוּא
לֵאמֹר: בַּעֲבוּר זֶה עָשָׂה יְיָ לִי בְּצֵאתִי
מִמִּצְרָיִם:

AND the one who doesn't know how to ask questions? Well, you'll have to open the conversation for him. Tell him things that will get him to ask. Tell him, "God did all these things for me in Egypt so that I would do all this stuff." Including stuff like trying to get you to ask questions.

You learn by asking questions—so the child with the brightest question comes first:

The Bright One

 *Someone else out loud:*

חָכָם מַה הוּא אוֹמֵר: מָה הָעֵדֹת וְהַחֻקִּים וְהַמִּשְׁפָּטִים אֲשֶׁר צִוָּה יְיָ אֱלֹהֵינוּ אֶתְכֶם. וְאַף אַתָּה אֱמֹר לוֹ כְּהִלְכוֹת הַפֶּסַח, אֵין מַפְטִירִין אַחַר הַפֶּסַח אֲפִיקוֹמָן:

WHAT does the bright one say?

"Explain to me all the symbolism, the rituals and the rules that God our God commanded you." So, besides telling him the story and all the explanations,[19] you also have to tell him all the rules of Passover, all the way to the last rule, that you don't eat anything after the Afikoman.

 WHAT'S INSIDE this child's question? Here are some possibilities:

1. This child is really excited about learning. That's real wisdom. So you teach.

2. This child doesn't get why we have to do all these rituals. If God is spiritual, then why don't we just philosophize and meditate?

   So you explain that God is beyond spiritual. You can't reach God with your mind, but you can be one with God by doing mitzvahs.

3. This child doesn't get how we could relate to a God who is way beyond any spiritual philosophizing or meditating. Why do we try to understand anything at all? Just do it!

So you explain that God wants us to connect to Him with every part of us, including our mind and heart. The ultimate point in the Seder is the taste of a matzah lingering in your mouth, symbolizing the delicious flavor of knowing what can't be known.[20]

The (Temporarily) Wicked One

 *Someone else out loud:*

רָשָׁע מַה הוּא אוֹמֵר: מָה הָעֲבֹדָה הַזֹּאת לָכֶם. לָכֶם וְלֹא לוֹ, וּלְפִי שֶׁהוֹצִיא אֶת עַצְמוֹ מִן הַכְּלָל, כָּפַר בְּעִקָּר. וְאַף אַתָּה הַקְהֵה אֶת שִׁנָּיו וֶאֱמֹר לוֹ: בַּעֲבוּר זֶה עָשָׂה יְיָ לִי בְּצֵאתִי מִמִּצְרַיִם, לִי וְלֹא לוֹ, אִלּוּ הָיָה שָׁם לֹא הָיָה נִגְאָל:

AS for the one who is (temporarily) wicked, what does he say? "Why do you people do all this?" He says "you people," excluding himself. He's denying the basis of the entire Seder—that we are one people. How can you celebrate Passover if there's no Jewish People? So you blunt his argument. You quote the verse, "It's because of this that God did all these things for me when I left Egypt." If he's excluding himself already, he's excluding himself from leaving Egypt. If he had been there, he would never have been liberated.

40

The Four Children at the Seder

Now, before we get to the Exodus story, here's a few lines similar to a blessing[14] before the mitzvah of telling the story. The Torah tells us this mitzvah four times, so there are four blessings in here:

 Everyone:

בָּרוּךְ הַמָּקוֹם, בָּרוּךְ הוּא, בָּרוּךְ שֶׁנָּתַן תּוֹרָה לְעַמּוֹ יִשְׂרָאֵל, בָּרוּךְ הוּא:

BLESSED is the One Who Encompasses the Entire World,[15] blessed be He. Blessed is the One who gave Torah to His people, blessed be He.

A lot of people like to sing these words:

**Bah-rookh hah-mah-kom, bah-rookh hoo!
Bah-rookh sheh-nah-tahn toh-rah
Leh-ah-moh yis-rah-ehl—bah-rookh hoo!**

 ALL OF A SUDDEN we're referring to God as the One Who Encompasses the Entire World. In Hebrew, that's just one word: *Hamakom*, The Place.

Why? Because, say the rabbis, the universe is not His place. Rather, He is the place of the universe. Which means that even as He is within time and space and all that happens there, He remains beyond it all.

And that's why we call Him by that title here:

If God belonged to some particular place, some of your children might be closer to Him and others further away. But since He encompasses everything and everyone, He's immediately accessible to all of us regardless of brains, personality type, or where we find ourselves in life.

The four kids of the Haggadah represent the gamut of human personality. And Torah has a particular approach for each one. Now that's wisdom from out of this world, in this world![16]

 *Someone out loud:*

כְּנֶגֶד אַרְבָּעָה בָנִים דִּבְּרָה תּוֹרָה: אֶחָד חָכָם, וְאֶחָד רָשָׁע, וְאֶחָד תָּם, וְאֶחָד שֶׁאֵינוֹ יוֹדֵעַ לִשְׁאוֹל:

THE Torah is so concerned that we get this story across, it tells four different ways to tell four different kinds of kids this story.

1. One is a bright, inquisitive kind of kid.
2. One is (temporarily[17]) wicked.
3. One is simple.
4 And one just doesn't know how to ask questions.[18]

IT TURNS OUT that the rabbis are also debating another important point: In the Messianic Era, will we still tell the miraculous story of how we left Egypt? Ben Zoma would tell you, "No way! After seeing the entire world enter an era of wisdom and peace, we will tell that story instead. As for miracles—we will be ever-aware of all the amazing miracles constantly surrounding us!"

But the rest of the rabbis disagree. They say that even after all the incredible miracles when we leave this final exile—way beyond the miracles of Egypt—we will still make mention of the Exodus from Egypt. Because that's when it all began.

As it turns out, that very day Ben Zoma (no, Ben wasn't his first name—that means "son of Zoma") had explained that there's an extra word here: It says "all the days of your life." There are plenty of other things the Torah tells me to remember, and it's self-understood that I have to remember it every day without being told so. If you don't remember every day, you're not remembering, you're forgetting, right?

So Ben Zoma came up with a simple formula:

> Days of your life = In the daytime, while the sun is shining.

> All the days of your life = In the daytime + the nighttime.

What about the rest of the rabbis? It seems they didn't have the same appreciation of Ben Zoma's insight. They provided a different formula:

> Days of your life = The life of this world.

> All the days of your life = The life of this world + the life of the world to come (a.k.a. the Messianic Era).

So, according to the rest of the rabbis, Ben Zoma has no proof from this verse.

How Five Big Rabbis Spent an Entire Night Doing This

Someone out loud:

מַ֫עֲשֶׂה בְּרַבִּי אֱלִיעֶ֫זֶר וְרַבִּי יְהוֹשֻׁ֫עַ וְרַבִּי אֶלְעָזָר בֶּן עֲזַרְיָה וְרַבִּי עֲקִיבָא וְרַבִּי טַרְפוֹן, שֶׁהָיוּ מְסֻבִּין בִּבְנֵי בְרַק, וְהָיוּ מְסַפְּרִים בִּיצִיאַת מִצְרַ֫יִם כָּל אוֹתוֹ הַלַּ֫יְלָה, עַד שֶׁבָּ֫אוּ תַלְמִידֵיהֶם וְאָמְרוּ לָהֶם: רַבּוֹתֵ֫ינוּ, הִגִּ֫יעַ זְמַן קְרִיאַת שְׁמַע שֶׁל שַׁחֲרִית:

JUST to give an example: There was an instance where five great rabbis were sitting at a Seder in B'nei Brak the whole night telling the story of the liberation from Egypt. Big rabbis: Rabbi Eliezer, Rabbi Yehoshua, Rabbi Elazar ben Azariah, Rabbi Akiva and Rabbi Tarfon.

They didn't stop until their students arrived and said, "Our teachers! It's already time to say the morning Shema!" (That's the "Hear O Israel, God is our God, God is One" that we say every morning and every night.)

אָמַר רַבִּי אֶלְעָזָר בֶּן עֲזַרְיָה: הֲרֵי אֲנִי כְּבֶן שִׁבְעִים שָׁנָה, וְלֹא זָכִ֫יתִי שֶׁתֵּאָמֵר יְצִיאַת מִצְרַ֫יִם בַּלֵּילוֹת, עַד שֶׁדְּרָשָׁהּ בֶּן זוֹמָא, שֶׁנֶּאֱמַר: לְמַ֫עַן תִּזְכֹּר אֶת יוֹם צֵאתְךָ מֵאֶ֫רֶץ מִצְרַ֫יִם כֹּל יְמֵי חַיֶּ֫יךָ. יְמֵי חַיֶּ֫יךָ הַיָּמִים, כֹּל יְמֵי חַיֶּ֫יךָ הַלֵּילוֹת. וַחֲכָמִים אוֹמְרִים: יְמֵי חַיֶּ֫יךָ הָעוֹלָם הַזֶּה, כֹּל יְמֵי חַיֶּ֫יךָ לְהָבִיא לִימוֹת הַמָּשִׁיחַ:

WHAT do you think they were discussing?

Well, for one thing, **Rabbi Elazar** pointed out that he was about seventy years old... well, he wasn't really—he was still a teenager—but he miraculously got this distinguished beard so that people would respect him when he was appointed head of the Supreme Court. So he looked seventy. And he had the wisdom of a seventy-year-old sage.

At any rate, Rabbi Elazar had not been able to figure out why we mention the Exodus not just every day, but also every night of the year.

Everything revolves around these words from the Torah:

"...in order that you should mention the Exodus from Egypt all the days of your life."

So since we did that already in the morning when we said the last paragraph of the Shema, why do we say that last paragraph again at night?

The Answer: Take One

Now we're about to start telling the story. The story is supposed to be told over matzah. So we uncover the matzah for all to see. The story is about God's love for us, how He carried us out of the humiliation of soul-crushing slavery to bring us close to Him. So we begin:

 Uncover the matzah.

עֲבָדִים הָיִינוּ לְפַרְעֹה בְּמִצְרָיִם, וַיּוֹצִיאֵנוּ יְיָ אֱלֹהֵינוּ מִשָּׁם בְּיָד חֲזָקָה וּבִזְרֹעַ נְטוּיָה, וְאִלּוּ לֹא הוֹצִיא הַקָּדוֹשׁ בָּרוּךְ הוּא אֶת אֲבוֹתֵינוּ מִמִּצְרַיִם, הֲרֵי אָנוּ וּבָנֵינוּ וּבְנֵי בָנֵינוּ מְשֻׁעְבָּדִים הָיִינוּ לְפַרְעֹה בְּמִצְרָיִם. וַאֲפִילוּ כֻּלָּנוּ חֲכָמִים כֻּלָּנוּ נְבוֹנִים כֻּלָּנוּ יוֹדְעִים אֶת הַתּוֹרָה, מִצְוָה עָלֵינוּ לְסַפֵּר בִּיצִיאַת מִצְרָיִם, וְכָל הַמַּרְבֶּה לְסַפֵּר בִּיצִיאַת מִצְרַיִם הֲרֵי זֶה מְשֻׁבָּח:

WE started off as slaves to the Pharaoh in Egypt. Until God liberated us from there with what's called "a strong hand and an outstretched arm"—basically, a lot of big miracles.

In fact, if He hadn't taken us out of there, we would be slaves, our children would be slaves, our grandchildren would be slaves...and so on. Nobody would even have thought of the whole idea of freedom.

That's why we're telling this story tonight.

Even if we would all be wise and understanding, even if we all knew everything that's written in the Torah, it would still be a mitzvah for us to tell this story tonight. And the more you tell of this story the better.

So if you have anything to add to what we're going to say, or any questions to ask, please speak up.

A lot of people like to sing these words:

**Ah-va-deem hah-yee-noo!
Leh-fah-roh beh-mitz-rah-yim!**

Now everyone can sing together the original Hebrew—even if you don't know Hebrew:

 Everyone:

**Mah nish-tah-nah hah-lai-lah hah-zeh
Mee-kohl hah-lay-loht?**

**Sheh-beh-khohl hah-lay-loht ayn ah-noo maht-bee-leen
Ah-fee-loo pah-ahm eh-khat,
Hah-lai-lah hah-zeh
Sheh-tay peh-ah-meem!**

**Sheh-beh-khohl hah-lay-loht ah-noo okh-leen
Kha-maytz o mah-tzah,
Hah-lai-lah hah-zeh
Koo-loh mah-tzah!**

**Sheh-beh-khohl hah-lay-loht ah-noo okh-leen
Sheh-ahr yeh-rah-koht,
Hah-lai-lah hah-zeh
Mah-rohr!**

**Sheh-beh-khohl hah-lay-loht ah-noo okh-leen
Bayn yoh-shveen oo-vayn meh-soo-been,
Hah-lai-lah hah-zeh
Koo-lah-noo meh-soo-been!**

Someone out loud (preferably a child):

מַה נִּשְׁתַּנָּה
הַלַּיְלָה הַזֶּה מִכָּל הַלֵּילוֹת.

שֶׁבְּכָל הַלֵּילוֹת אֵין אָנוּ מַטְבִּילִין אֲפִילוּ פַּעַם אֶחָת, הַלַּיְלָה הַזֶּה שְׁתֵּי פְעָמִים:

שֶׁבְּכָל הַלֵּילוֹת אָנוּ אוֹכְלִין חָמֵץ אוֹ מַצָּה, הַלַּיְלָה הַזֶּה כֻּלּוֹ מַצָּה:

שֶׁבְּכָל הַלֵּילוֹת אָנוּ אוֹכְלִין שְׁאָר יְרָקוֹת, הַלַּיְלָה הַזֶּה מָרוֹר:

שֶׁבְּכָל הַלֵּילוֹת אָנוּ אוֹכְלִין בֵּין יוֹשְׁבִין וּבֵין מְסֻבִּין, הַלַּיְלָה הַזֶּה כֻּלָּנוּ מְסֻבִּין:

I'VE got four questions to ask.

Basically, I want to know:

What makes tonight different than every other night?

1. On other nights we don't go dipping vegetables before we start the meal.[11] But tonight, we do, so we end up dipping twice! One time in saltwater, and once in the charoset!

2. On other nights we can eat chametz or we can eat matzah. Tonight, everything is matzah!

3. On other nights, we eat all sorts of vegetables. Tonight, we make a big deal out of eating a bitter vegetable!

4. On other nights, we sit or we lean. Tonight, when we drink wine or eat matzah, everyone's leaning!

THE ORDER of the four questions is not the same in every Haggadah. But you can't go wrong with any version. This one is found in the Jerusalem Talmud, in the first printed Haggadah, and in almost all the early authorities.

And according to Kabbalah, it lines up with the order of the four worlds, beginning with our world and working up through the higher, spiritual worlds.

It also makes a lot of sense, because it follows the actual order of these things as they catch a kid's attention tonight.

That just goes to show how vital all these little details of the Seder are, even the customs that aren't mentioned in Torah—because it's those micro-rituals that spark the kids' interest and stay with them for life![12]

Nevertheless, it's not that any other order is wrong. Originally you didn't have to ask specifically these questions. Maybe the kids would come up with other questions![13]

Mah Nishtanah
The Four Questions

 IN MANY HOMES, everyone begins this by saying, "Dad/Tatte/Abba, I want to ask you four questions." Even if they don't have a dad there.

Because the Haggadah is described in the Torah as an answer to a child's question. After all, children get what you're telling them only when it answers their question.

In case the children have no questions, we provide four right here. But really, we are all children tonight. We are all reborn, leaving our own Egypt. And who do we ask? Dad. Our ultimate Dad.

On the night of Passover, a Jew sits with the Creator of the Universe and says, "Dad, I want to ask you a few questions: Why is this night different from any other night? Meaning: Why is this darkness different from any other darkness? Why did You abandon us to this exile for almost 2,000 years? Why all this bitterness?"

And then, as is the responsibility of every parent on the night of Passover, the Creator of the Universe must respond.

He must respond that on this night He is going to take each of us by the hand and schlep us out of our personal Egypt, and the whole world out of its darkness.

And then we will see that the darkness was all worthwhile, really worthwhile.[10]

Magid מַגִּיד

Tell the Story

Introducing Matzah

Now it's time to formally introduce the centerpiece of our celebrations tonight, the humble matzah. So we uncover the matzah a little for all to see, and then we all say or sing:

הָא לַחְמָא עַנְיָא דִּי אֲכָלוּ אַבְהָתָנָא בְּאַרְעָא דְמִצְרָיִם. כָּל דִּכְפִין יֵיתֵי וְיֵכֹל, כָּל דִּצְרִיךְ יֵיתֵי וְיִפְסַח. הַשַּׁתָּא הָכָא, לְשָׁנָה הַבָּאָה בְּאַרְעָא דְיִשְׂרָאֵל. הַשַּׁתָּא עַבְדִין, לְשָׁנָה הַבָּאָה בְּנֵי חוֹרִין:

THIS is the bread of affliction that our ancestors ate in the land of Egypt. Whoever is hungry, come eat with us! Whoever is needy, come join our Seder! This year we're here; next year in the land of Israel! This year we're slaves; next year we will be free!

THIS MAY SEEM A LITTLE BIZARRE. We came to celebrate our freedom, and here we are saying that we're still slaves. So what are we celebrating?

The truth is, the Exodus never really accomplished all of its goals. A lot of things never went as planned. And so, eventually we ended back up in exile.

That's how it goes with top-down relief projects. If you want to make lasting change, it's got to come from within the people.

And that's precisely what we are planning to do tonight: We're going to liberate ourselves from our own private exiles, and thereby facilitate the Exodus of the entire world. How? By doing the mitzvahs of the Seder from a place deep inside.[8]

Pour the Second Cup

Now cover the matzah for the Four Questions. Then everyone refills their cup.

This is the cup over which we tell the Exodus story.

YOU'RE PROBABLY ASKING, "Why do we cover the matzah? And why pour the cup now? Why not wait until we're going to drink it?"

Well, it's because if nothing else got the kids to ask questions until now, for sure this will. Look, it worked for you![9]

Yachatz

Break the Middle Matzah

We need to tell the story with matzah on the table. But it has to be matzah that's not whole. That's what the Torah calls "bread of suffering," reminiscent of the suffering of Egyptian slavery.[4] So:

1. Grasp the middle matzah.

2. Break it in half (while it's still covered).[5]

3. Leave the smaller half between the two other matzahs. This is the matzah over which the Haggadah is recited. (The other two matzahs are there because we always use two whole loaves at Shabbat and holiday meals.)[6]

4. The larger piece is called the Afikoman (which basically means "dessert"). Keep it somewhere safe. You'll need it at the end of the meal.

- Many Ashkenazic Jews have the custom of hiding the Afikoman. Later, when the kids are restless, you can offer them a reward for finding it. Others do the reverse: The kids hide it and the adults have to find it.

- An ancient custom of many Middle-Eastern Jews: Wrap the pieces in napkins, then in a scarf. Then wrap the scarf over the shoulders of the children, so that the matzah is under their arms. Tell them that they are the Children of Israel, carrying the matzah out of Egypt.

Here's a fun idea. Ask everyone to vote on which piece is bigger and which piece is smaller.

THE CUSTOM of the Rebbe Rashab, Rabbi Sholom DovBer Schneersohn (1860–1920), the fifth Rebbe of Lubavitch, was to break the larger (Afikoman) piece into five pieces. That's very Kabbalistic. You see, God created the world with divine speech. But wait: God speaks? He's not a person with a mouth or a larynx. How does He speak?

Well, He brings His thoughts into reality—just like we bring our thoughts to other people with our speech. Except that His thoughts actually become real. We coordinate our throat, tongue, palate, teeth and lips—five different devices—to divide up a simple breath into many different sounds. That's because God designed us to mirror His mode of talking. He uses five basic means to divide His divine creative energy into the infinite articulations that create everything in the universe.

Our job is to reconnect all things back to their origin, as they are all united within that divine energy, before they were divided up. That's what we accomplish with every mitzvah we do in this world. And that's reflected in breaking the Afikoman into five pieces, hiding them, then bringing them out and eating them.[7]

Urchatz / וּרְחַץ

Wash hands, no blessing

I know, you just sat down. But now you're going to have to stand up. Why? Because now we all have to go to the sink to wash our hands. Your hands are clean already? You sterilized them before the meal? Sorry, not good enough. This is a ritual hand-washing we do before eating anything dipped in water, as a way of remembering the rules of purity kept in Temple times. Some bring a basin to the table and let people wash there.

Pour water on each hand three times using a washing cup, covering the entire hand each time, from the wrist to the fingertips.
Usually there's a blessing recited—but not this time. Make sure no one says the blessing by mistake.

Karpas / כַּרְפַּס

Eat a Vegetable

Take a small piece (up to half an ounce, smaller than an olive) of whatever vegetable you're using for Karpas. Dip it into the saltwater. You need to say a blessing over it, just like with any other piece of food. But have in mind that this blessing also covers the bitter herbs you'll be eating later on. Now say the blessing:

 Everyone:

בָּרוּךְ אַתָּה יְיָ, אֱלֹהֵינוּ מֶלֶךְ הָעוֹלָם, בּוֹרֵא פְּרִי הָאֲדָמָה:

BLESSED are You, God our God, King of the universe, who creates the fruit of the earth.

Bah-rookh ah-tah ah-doh-noi eh-loh-hay-noo meh-lekh hah-oh-lahm boh-ray pree hah-ah-dah-mah.

And munch.

 NOW, YOU MAY ASK, why did we do that right after Kiddush?

We did that so that someone would ask why we did that right after Kiddush. After all, it's not the usual order to begin a meal with a tiny snack. Usually you go straight for the bread. To which the answer is: So that someone will ask why we did that.

Because, tonight, people are supposed to ask questions. Especially children. And, even if we don't have answers to all the questions, we can tell the story as an answer to a lot of questions.³ Because when a story answers a question, it's a story that's remembered.

KADESH

Now say the Havdalah blessing:

בָּרוּךְ אַתָּה יְיָ, אֱלֹהֵינוּ מֶלֶךְ הָעוֹלָם, הַמַּבְדִּיל בֵּין קֹדֶשׁ לְחוֹל, בֵּין אוֹר לְחֹשֶׁךְ, בֵּין יִשְׂרָאֵל לָעַמִּים, בֵּין יוֹם הַשְּׁבִיעִי לְשֵׁשֶׁת יְמֵי הַמַּעֲשֶׂה. בֵּין קְדֻשַּׁת שַׁבָּת לִקְדֻשַּׁת יוֹם טוֹב הִבְדַּלְתָּ, וְאֶת יוֹם הַשְּׁבִיעִי מִשֵּׁשֶׁת יְמֵי הַמַּעֲשֶׂה קִדַּשְׁתָּ, הִבְדַּלְתָּ וְקִדַּשְׁתָּ אֶת עַמְּךָ יִשְׂרָאֵל בִּקְדֻשָּׁתֶךָ: בָּרוּךְ אַתָּה יְיָ, הַמַּבְדִּיל בֵּין קֹדֶשׁ לְקֹדֶשׁ:

BLESSED are You, God, our God, King of the universe, who makes the sacred distinct from the profane, the light from darkness, Israel from the nations, the seventh day from the six workdays. You have made the holiness of the Shabbat distinct from the holiness of the festival, and You have sanctified the seventh day above the six workdays. You have set apart Your people Israel and made them holy with Your holiness. Blessed are You, God, who makes a distinction between one kind of holiness and another kind of holiness.

Don't say this if you already said it when lighting the holiday candles:

בָּרוּךְ אַתָּה יְיָ, אֱלֹהֵינוּ מֶלֶךְ הָעוֹלָם, שֶׁהֶחֱיָנוּ וְקִיְּמָנוּ וְהִגִּיעָנוּ לַזְּמַן הַזֶּה:

BLESSED are You, God, our God, King of the universe, who has granted us life, sustained us, and gotten us all the way to this point in time!

If you want to say this blessing like a pro:

Bah-rookh ah-tah ah-doh-noi eh-loh-hay-noo meh-lekh hah-oh-lahm sheh-heh-kheh-yah-noo veh-kee-yeh-mah-noo veh-hig-ee-ah-noo liz-mahn hah-zeh.

 Now sit, lean to the left, and drink your first of the four cups of wine!

Kiddush for the Seder on Saturday night:

אַתְקִינוּ סְעוּדָתָא דְמַלְכָּא עִלָּאָה, דָּא הִיא סְעוּדָתָא דְקוּדְשָׁא בְּרִיךְ הוּא וּשְׁכִינְתֵּיהּ:

PREPARE the feast of the supernal King! This is the feast of the Holy One, may He be blessed, and His Shechinah.

 Make sure it's after nightfall. Everyone stands up, their full cup in hand, and says:

 Someone out loud or everyone

סַבְרִי מָרָנָן:

Attention Everybody!

בָּרוּךְ אַתָּה יְיָ, אֱלֹהֵינוּ מֶלֶךְ הָעוֹלָם, בּוֹרֵא פְּרִי הַגָּפֶן:

BLESSED are You, God, our God, King of the universe, who creates the fruit of the vine.

If you want to say that first blessing like a pro:

Bah-rookh ah-tah ah-doh-noi eh-loh-hay-noo meh-lekh hah-oh-lahm boh-ray pree hah-gah-fehn.

בָּרוּךְ אַתָּה יְיָ, אֱלֹהֵינוּ מֶלֶךְ הָעוֹלָם, אֲשֶׁר בָּחַר בָּנוּ מִכָּל עָם, וְרוֹמְמָנוּ מִכָּל לָשׁוֹן, וְקִדְּשָׁנוּ בְּמִצְוֹתָיו. וַתִּתֶּן לָנוּ יְיָ אֱלֹהֵינוּ בְּאַהֲבָה מוֹעֲדִים לְשִׂמְחָה, חַגִּים וּזְמַנִּים לְשָׂשׂוֹן, אֶת יוֹם חַג הַמַּצּוֹת הַזֶּה, וְאֶת יוֹם טוֹב מִקְרָא קֹדֶשׁ הַזֶּה, זְמַן חֵרוּתֵנוּ, מִקְרָא קֹדֶשׁ, זֵכֶר לִיצִיאַת מִצְרָיִם. כִּי בָנוּ בָחַרְתָּ וְאוֹתָנוּ קִדַּשְׁתָּ מִכָּל הָעַמִּים, וּמוֹעֲדֵי קָדְשֶׁךָ בְּשִׂמְחָה וּבְשָׂשׂוֹן הִנְחַלְתָּנוּ: בָּרוּךְ אַתָּה יְיָ, מְקַדֵּשׁ יִשְׂרָאֵל וְהַזְּמַנִּים:

BLESSED are You, God, our God, King of the universe, who has chosen us from among all people, and raised us above all tongues, and made us holy through His mitzvahs.

And You, God, our God, have lovingly given us festivals for happiness, feasts and festive seasons for rejoicing! This day of the matzah feast and this day to be called holy, the season of our freedom, to be called holy, commemorating the Exodus from Egypt.

For You have chosen us and sanctified us from all the nations, and You gave us Your festivals as a heritage in happiness and in joy.

Blessed are You, God, who sanctifies Israel and the festive seasons!

On Saturday night, after Shabbat departs, we say Havdalah—to make a distinction between Shabbat and the holiday.

Glance at the holiday candles, then say this blessing:

בָּרוּךְ אַתָּה יְיָ, אֱלֹהֵינוּ מֶלֶךְ הָעוֹלָם, בּוֹרֵא מְאוֹרֵי הָאֵשׁ:

BLESSED are You, God, our God, King of the universe, who creates the lights of fire.

אֶת יוֹם הַשַּׁבָּת הַזֶּה וְאֶת יוֹם חַג הַמַּצּוֹת הַזֶּה, וְאֶת יוֹם טוֹב מִקְרָא קֹדֶשׁ הַזֶּה, זְמַן חֵרוּתֵנוּ, בְּאַהֲבָה מִקְרָא קֹדֶשׁ, זֵכֶר לִיצִיאַת מִצְרָיִם. כִּי בָנוּ בָחַרְתָּ וְאוֹתָנוּ קִדַּשְׁתָּ מִכָּל הָעַמִּים, וְשַׁבָּת וּמוֹעֲדֵי קָדְשֶׁךָ בְּאַהֲבָה וּבְרָצוֹן בְּשִׂמְחָה וּבְשָׂשׂוֹן הִנְחַלְתָּנוּ: בָּרוּךְ אַתָּה יְיָ, מְקַדֵּשׁ הַשַּׁבָּת וְיִשְׂרָאֵל וְהַזְּמַנִּים:

This Shabbat day and this day of the Matzot feast and this day to be called holy, the season of our freedom, in love, to be called holy, commemorating the Exodus from Egypt.

For You have chosen and sanctified us from all the nations, and You have given us Your holy Shabbat and festivals as a heritage in love and favor, in happiness and in joy.

Blessed are You, God, who sanctifies the Shabbat and Israel and the festive seasons!

Don't say this if you already said it when lighting the holiday candles:

בָּרוּךְ אַתָּה יְיָ, אֱלֹהֵינוּ מֶלֶךְ הָעוֹלָם, שֶׁהֶחֱיָנוּ וְקִיְּמָנוּ וְהִגִּיעָנוּ לַזְּמַן הַזֶּה:

BLESSED are You, God, our God, King of the universe, who has granted us life, sustained us, and gotten us all the way to this point in time!

If you want to say this blessing like a pro:

Bah-rookh ah-tah ah-doh-noi eh-loh-hay-noo meh-lekh hah-oh-lahm sheh-heh-kheh-yah-noo veh-kee-yeh-mah-noo veh-hig-ee-ah-noo liz-mahn hah-zeh.

 Now sit, lean to the left and drink your first of four cups of wine!

Kiddush for the Seder on Friday night:

Make sure it's after nightfall. You'll find the songs, including Shalom Aleichem, that customarily precede Kiddush on Friday night on page 104.

Everyone stands up, their full cup in hand, and says:

 Someone out loud or everyone

יוֹם הַשִּׁשִּׁי: וַיְכֻלּוּ הַשָּׁמַיִם וְהָאָרֶץ וְכָל צְבָאָם:

וַיְכַל אֱלֹהִים בַּיּוֹם הַשְּׁבִיעִי מְלַאכְתּוֹ אֲשֶׁר עָשָׂה, וַיִּשְׁבֹּת בַּיּוֹם הַשְּׁבִיעִי מִכָּל מְלַאכְתּוֹ אֲשֶׁר עָשָׂה:

וַיְבָרֶךְ אֱלֹהִים אֶת יוֹם הַשְּׁבִיעִי וַיְקַדֵּשׁ אֹתוֹ, כִּי בוֹ שָׁבַת מִכָּל מְלַאכְתּוֹ אֲשֶׁר בָּרָא אֱלֹהִים לַעֲשׂוֹת:

THE sixth day.

The heavens and the earth and everything that populates them were complete.

And with the seventh day, God completed His work which He had made. So He rested on the seventh day from all His work which He had made.

Then God blessed the seventh day and made it holy, for on it He rested from all His work which God had already created to be done.

סַבְרִי מָרָנָן:

בָּרוּךְ אַתָּה יְיָ, אֱלֹהֵינוּ מֶלֶךְ הָעוֹלָם, בּוֹרֵא פְּרִי הַגָּפֶן:

Attention Everybody!

BLESSED are You, God, our God, King of the universe, who creates the fruit of the vine.

If you want to say that first blessing like a pro:

Bah-rookh ah-tah ah-doh-noi eh-loh-hay-noo meh-lekh hah-oh-lahm boh-ray pree hah-gah-fehn.

בָּרוּךְ אַתָּה יְיָ, אֱלֹהֵינוּ מֶלֶךְ הָעוֹלָם, אֲשֶׁר בָּחַר בָּנוּ מִכָּל עָם, וְרוֹמְמָנוּ מִכָּל לָשׁוֹן, וְקִדְּשָׁנוּ בְּמִצְוֹתָיו.

וַתִּתֶּן לָנוּ יְיָ אֱלֹהֵינוּ בְּאַהֲבָה שַׁבָּתוֹת לִמְנוּחָה וּמוֹעֲדִים לְשִׂמְחָה, חַגִּים וּזְמַנִּים לְשָׂשׂוֹן,

BLESSED are You, God, our God, King of the universe, who has chosen us from among all people, raised us above all tongues, and sanctified us through His mitzvahs.

And You, God, our God, have given us in love Shabbats for rest and festivals for happiness, feasts and festive seasons for rejoicing!

Kiddush when the Seder is not on a Friday or Saturday night:

You'll find the Kiddush for those days on the next pages.

אַתְקִינוּ סְעוּדָתָא דְמַלְכָּא עִלָּאָה, דָּא הִיא סְעוּדָתָא דְקוּדְשָׁא בְּרִיךְ הוּא וּשְׁכִינְתֵּיהּ:

PREPARE the feast of the supernal King! This is the feast of the Holy One, may He be blessed, and His Shechinah.

 Make sure it's after nightfall. Everyone stands up, their full cup in hand, and says:

 Someone out loud or everyone

סַבְרִי מָרָנָן:

Attention Everybody!

בָּרוּךְ אַתָּה יְיָ, אֱלֹהֵינוּ מֶלֶךְ הָעוֹלָם, בּוֹרֵא פְּרִי הַגָּפֶן:

BLESSED are You, God, our God, King of the universe, who creates the fruit of the vine.

If you want to say that first blessing like a pro:

Bah-rookh ah-tah ah-doh-noi eh-loh-hay-noo meh-lekh hah-oh-lahm boh-ray pree hah-gah-fehn.

בָּרוּךְ אַתָּה יְיָ, אֱלֹהֵינוּ מֶלֶךְ הָעוֹלָם, אֲשֶׁר בָּחַר בָּנוּ מִכָּל עָם, וְרוֹמְמָנוּ מִכָּל לָשׁוֹן, וְקִדְּשָׁנוּ בְּמִצְוֹתָיו. וַתִּתֶּן לָנוּ יְיָ אֱלֹהֵינוּ בְּאַהֲבָה מוֹעֲדִים לְשִׂמְחָה, חַגִּים וּזְמַנִּים לְשָׂשׂוֹן, אֶת יוֹם חַג הַמַּצוֹת הַזֶּה, וְאֶת יוֹם טוֹב מִקְרָא קֹדֶשׁ הַזֶּה, זְמַן חֵרוּתֵנוּ, מִקְרָא קֹדֶשׁ, זֵכֶר לִיצִיאַת מִצְרָיִם. כִּי בָנוּ בָחַרְתָּ וְאוֹתָנוּ קִדַּשְׁתָּ מִכָּל הָעַמִּים, וּמוֹעֲדֵי קָדְשֶׁךָ בְּשִׂמְחָה וּבְשָׂשׂוֹן הִנְחַלְתָּנוּ: בָּרוּךְ אַתָּה יְיָ, מְקַדֵּשׁ יִשְׂרָאֵל וְהַזְּמַנִּים:

BLESSED are You, God, our God, King of the universe, who has chosen us from among all people, and raised us above all tongues, and made us holy through His mitzvahs. And You, God, our God, have lovingly given us festivals for happiness, feasts and festive seasons for rejoicing! This day of the matzah feast and this day to be called holy, the season of our freedom, to be called holy, commemorating the Exodus from Egypt.

For You have chosen us and sanctified us from all the nations, and You gave us Your holy festivals as a heritage in happiness and in joy.

Blessed are You, God, who sanctifies Israel and the festive seasons!

Don't say this if you already said it when lighting the holiday candles:

בָּרוּךְ אַתָּה יְיָ, אֱלֹהֵינוּ מֶלֶךְ הָעוֹלָם, שֶׁהֶחֱיָנוּ וְקִיְּמָנוּ וְהִגִּיעָנוּ לַזְּמַן הַזֶּה:

BLESSED are You, God, our God, King of the universe, who has granted us life, sustained us, and gotten us all the way to this point in time!

If you want to say this blessing like a pro:

Bah-rookh ah-tah ah-doh-noi eh-loh-hay-noo meh-lekh hah-oh-lahm sheh-heh-kheh-yah-noo veh-kee-yeh-mah-noo veh-hig-ee-ah-noo liz-mahn hah-zeh.

 Now sit, lean to the left and drink your first of the four cups of wine!

 Kadesh

Kiddush on Wine

JUST LIKE OUR ancestors had to first leave Egypt before they could get the Torah, we first have to leave behind the busy, buzzing hullabaloo of the world so we can enter a timeless time. A space where all of us, our great-grandparents, our ancestors who left Egypt and every last Jew that lives, has lived or will live, all live all at once, as a single person.

How are we going to enter that space?

With a full cup of wine.

Wine is tonight's representative of freedom, so freely fill your cup to the brim.

On other nights, one person makes Kiddush and everyone else gets a sip. Tonight is different. Everyone gets their own cup, and everyone drinks it down. Because this is cup #1 of tonight's obligatory four cups.

Make sure each cup holds at least three ounces (86 ml).

At the end of Kiddush, sit down, lean to your left, and drink the whole cup. If that's too much, then most of the cup. Well, at least enough wine to fill one cheek. For most of us, that's about one and a half ounces (45 ml).

THE TORAH doesn't prescribe four cups of wine, but the rabbis did—and the Torah says we should listen to our sages. But why four cups?

The clue is in a passage in which God promises Moses that He's about to initiate the rescue operation from Egypt:

*So now tell the Jewish People, I'm God and I keep My promises. So I'm about to **extract** you from the hardships of Egypt. I'm about to **rescue** you from laboring for these guys. I'm about to **liberate** you with an outstretched arm and major judgments of these people. And then I'm going to **marry** you as My people, and I will be your God.*

See those four verbs: Extract, Rescue, Liberate, Marry (the actual wording is "take to Me," but that's what those words usually mean—marriage). That's the order of exodus and liberation for the Jewish People. It's also the four stages for any person who wants to get out of a rut and rise higher.

First you need to extract yourself out of the lousy place you fell into—just get out of there. Then you need to work on rescuing yourself from its influence and power over you.

Next comes real freedom and liberation by immersing yourself in Torah wisdom, mitzvahs and good deeds. And the ultimate destiny of all of Torah is oneness with the one God, like a marriage.

So we celebrate and experience each of those vital stages of liberation by drinking each of these four cups at the appropriate stage in the Seder.

Make sure to pour each of them and drink these cups at the right point in the Seder, because otherwise they just aren't the four cups the sages prescribed.[2]

The Passover Seder

Tonight's Program

In many homes, this is sung before Kiddush:

Someone out loud or everyone:

Transliteration	Hebrew	Rap Version
Kadaysh	קַדֵּשׁ	Kiddush on wine,
Urchatz	וּרְחַץ	wash hands, no brachah.
Karpas	כַּרְפַּס	Eat a vegetable,
Yachatz	יַחַץ	break a matzah.
Magid	מַגִּיד	Tell the story,
Rachtza	רָחְצָה	wash hands with a brachah.
Motzi	מוֹצִיא	Blessing on the matzah,
Matzah	מַצָּה	blessing on the mitzvah.
Maror	מָרוֹר	Bitter leaves for eating,
Koraych	כּוֹרֵךְ	bitter in a wrapping.
Shulchan Oraych	שֻׁלְחָן עוֹרֵךְ	Now it's time for eating. Now it's time for drinking.
Tzafun	צָפוּן	Eat the afikoman,
Bayrach	בָּרֵךְ	thank God for everything.
Hallel	הַלֵּל	Praise God for His wonders!
Nirtzah	נִרְצָה	He accepts—despite our blunders.

While we're discussing requirements, here are the basics of what we need to get done tonight:

1. Tell the story of the Exodus, miracles included.
2. Eat a bitter vegetable.
3. Eat matzah—lots of it. Well, at the very least, half a typical handmade shmurah matzah or a whole machine matzah.
4. Eat a meal.
5. Drink four cups of kosher wine at set times in the Seder.
6. Sing songs of praise to God for His wonders.

  ...and don't start any of it until after nightfall, like it says, "You shall tell your child on that night."

The Seder Plate

How to Set Up the Seder Plate

First arrange three whole matzahs on a plate, one on top of the other, with a cloth or napkin between each one. Then, on the cloth or plate above all the matzahs, place these items*:

Start with the Zeroa (#1) on the top right, then place the Baytza (#2) on the top left, then the Maror (#3) in the middle. The same with the next three: Right, left, middle.

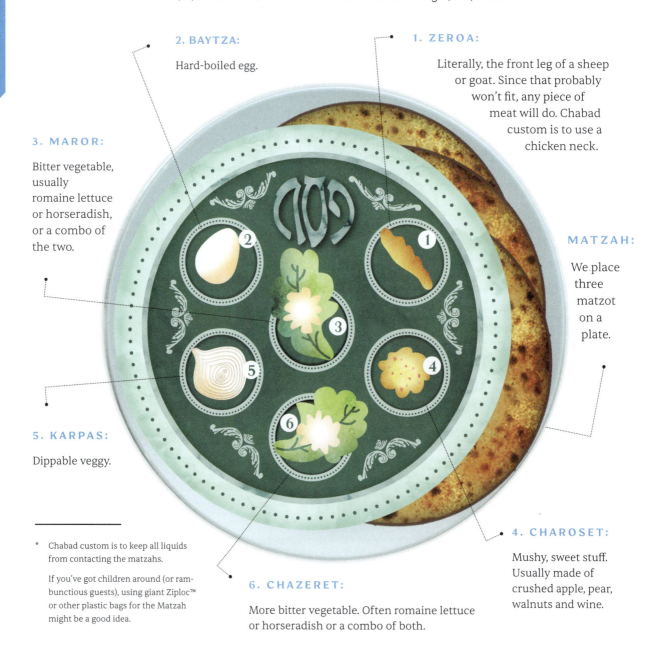

2. BAYTZA:
Hard-boiled egg.

1. ZEROA:
Literally, the front leg of a sheep or goat. Since that probably won't fit, any piece of meat will do. Chabad custom is to use a chicken neck.

3. MAROR:
Bitter vegetable, usually romaine lettuce or horseradish, or a combo of the two.

MATZAH:
We place three matzot on a plate.

5. KARPAS:
Dippable veggy.

6. CHAZERET:
More bitter vegetable. Often romaine lettuce or horseradish or a combo of both.

4. CHAROSET:
Mushy, sweet stuff. Usually made of crushed apple, pear, walnuts and wine.

---

* Chabad custom is to keep all liquids from contacting the matzahs.

If you've got children around (or rambunctious guests), using giant Ziploc™ or other plastic bags for the Matzah might be a good idea.

Candle Lighting

Before starting the Seder, all women and girls light candles and say a blessing. Married women generally light two candles. Many women light one candle for each child as well. Young girls should light and say a blessing before their mothers so that their mothers can assist them.

If it's Friday night, light the candles at least 18 minutes before sunset. Once the sun has set, it's Shabbat, and handling fire is forbidden. For the same reason, if it's Saturday night, don't light candles until it's dark and Shabbat is over.

On Yom Tov, unlike Shabbat, you can transfer fire—but you can't make a new fire. So, in order to light candles on Yom Tov, you will need to have another flame lit before the festival that will last until the second night. (When Passover begins on Saturday night, you'll need to keep a flame burning from Friday pre-sunset until Sunday night.)

On the first night, if it's not Shabbat, give at least a few coins to charity before lighting candles. But once the sun has set and it's Yom Tov or Shabbat, handling money is forbidden

> Light the candle(s). Now draw your hands over the flames and towards yourself to cover your eyes. Then recite the following two blessings:

On Friday night, add the words in shaded parentheses.

בָּרוּךְ אַתָּה יְיָ, אֱלֹהֵינוּ מֶלֶךְ הָעוֹלָם, אֲשֶׁר קִדְּשָׁנוּ בְּמִצְוֹתָיו, וְצִוָּנוּ לְהַדְלִיק נֵר שֶׁל (שַׁבָּת וְשֶׁל) יוֹם טוֹב:

BLESSED are You, God, our God, King of the universe, who has made us holy with His mitzvahs, and commanded us to light the candles of (Shabbat and of) Yom Tov.

Bah-rookh ah-tah ah-doh-noi eh-loh-hay-noo meh-lekh hah-oh-lahm ah-sher ki-deh-shah-noo beh-mitz-voh-tahv veh-tzee-vah-noo leh-hahd-lik nayr shehl (shah-baht veh-shehl) yohm tohv.

בָּרוּךְ אַתָּה יְיָ, אֱלֹהֵינוּ מֶלֶךְ הָעוֹלָם, שֶׁהֶחֱיָנוּ וְקִיְּמָנוּ וְהִגִּיעָנוּ לִזְמַן הַזֶּה:

BLESSED are You, God, our God, King of the universe, who has granted us life, sustained us, and gotten us all the way to this point in time!

Bah-rookh ah-tah ah-doh-noi eh-loh-hay-noo meh-lekh hah-oh-lahm sheh-heh-kheh-yah-noo veh-kee-yeh-mah-noo veh-hig-ee-ah-noo liz-mahn hah-zeh.

What You'll Need for the Seder

The centerpiece of the Seder table is the plate over which the Haggadah is said. There are different ways to organize this Seder plate, the setup offered on page 21 is according to Rabbi Isaac Luria (a.k.a. the Arizal).

We're all going to drink **four cups of wine**, and best if you drink all, or at least most, of your cup each time. So some people might want a smaller cup—but don't go any smaller than three ounces. And make sure to have lots of wine ready. (If they really don't like wine, you can provide grape juice, but it's a good idea to add a little wine to the mix if they're okay with that.)

Of course, the star of the show is the **matzah**. So use the real thing—get round, hand-baked shmurah matzah. You'll need to pile up three of them, with a napkin or cloth between each one. Many keep them all inside a special covering.

Make sure you have enough matzah for everyone to eat. At the very least, half a handmade shmurah matzah per person, or one whole machine-made matzah. Better to double that, or more.

It's best to eat your final matzah (the Afikoman) on the first night before midnight. Midnight is not necessarily 12 AM. During daylight savings time, it's more like 1 AM—give or take according to your longitude.

So it's a good idea to look up the precise time for midnight in your location at:

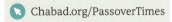 Chabad.org/PassoverTimes

On page 21, you'll see how to set the Seder plate. Make sure you have enough of everything that's there, so that everyone will have enough to partake.

You will need a **Zeroa**, literally, the front leg of a sheep or goat. Since that probably won't fit on the Seder plate, any piece of meat will do. Chabad custom is to use a broiled chicken neck.

You also need a **Baytza**, that's a hard-boiled egg.

For **Maror/Chazeret**, the bitter vegetable, that's 1.22 ounces (34 grams) per person, for two servings each. Chabad custom is to use romaine lettuce or horseradish or a combo of both. Horseradish is used only if it's unadulterated—not pickled or sweetened. Which means you might have to purchase a root and grind it yourself (a hands-on bitter labor experience!).

Then there's the **Charoset**, mushy sweet stuff usually made of crushed apple, pear, walnuts and wine.

> Find plenty of Charoset recipes at Chabad.org/Charoset.

You'll also need to prepare a dippable vegetable for **Karpas**, such as parsley (flat-leaf parsley should be checked for bugs), celery, or carrot sticks. Chabad custom is to use a raw onion or cooked potato. You'll need a bowl of saltwater, as well, to dip this into. (If the Seder is on Friday night, prepare your saltwater before Shabbat.)

There's also a pillow at everyone's chair, since we're celebrating freedom, and free people have a right to be comfortable. We'll also use our pillow throughout the Seder when the instructions call for us to lean while drinking or eating.

For the meal, many communities have a custom not to eat roast meat. And talking about meals, it's a good idea to warn your guests that you won't be starting the meal for a while—that way they won't arrive starving hungry.

Of course, the most important thing you'll need for the Seder are people who can say, "If God hadn't taken our ancestors out of Egypt, we and our children and our grandchildren would still be slaves."

In other words, you need people who left Egypt almost three and a half thousand years ago. You need Jews. Get as many as you can.

Pre-Passover Shopping List

- ☐ Lots of kosher for Passover food.
  - 🖱 For tons of kosher for Passover recipes, go to Chabad.org/PassoverRecipes.
- ☐ Lots of wine and/or grape juice.
- ☐ Lots of kosher for Passover matzah. (See the Matzah section above.)
- ☐ Candles for two nights (make that three nights, if Passover starts on Saturday night).
- ☐ 48-hour candle, so you can light your Yom Tov candles on the second night.*
- ☐ Cooked or broiled chicken neck for the Seder plate. (See Zeroa on facing page.)
- ☐ Hard-boiled eggs for the Seder plate.
- ☐ Raw horseradish (enough for everyone).
- ☐ Lots of Romaine lettuce.
- ☐ Apples, pears and walnuts for charoset.
- ☐ Vegetable (like raw onion, celery, parsley, baby carrots or cooked potato...) for dipping.
- ☐ Big plates for Seder plates.
- ☐ Matzah covers. You can purchase elegant triple-decker ones.
- ☐ Cups or glasses for everyone, holding at least three ounces.
- ☐ A bowl, preferably a little broken, for pouring the wine into from your cups.
- ☐ Purchase or print out copies of this Haggadah.

---

* Since you can't light fire on Shabbat or Yom Tov, you'll need to light a candle that will last more than 25 hours before sunset on the first night of the holiday. Then, on the second night, you can use its flame to light the Yom Tov candles. (Although you can't transfer a flame on Shabbat, on Yom Tov it's permissible.)

When Passover starts on Saturday night, you'll need to light a 72-hour candle on Friday before sundown. Then, use its flame to light the candles on Saturday and Sunday nights.

HANDMADE SHMURAH MATZAH

For the Seder, you want matzah that was made specifically for the mitzvah of eating matzah at the Seder—and we haven't yet invented machines that can have that in mind. So the ultimate matzah is made by hand in a bakery where everyone yells out "For the sake of the mitzvah of matzah!" before kneading, rolling, or baking the dough.

Recently, handmade shmurah matzah has become available through several major grocery outlets, as well as online. Your local Chabad Center will likely also have some.

> Go to Chabad.org/265986 for more purchase options.

Get the Details

- The only time you have to eat matzah is on the two Seder nights (in Israel, just the first night).
- For those folks with wheat allergies, gluten intolerance or celiac disease, read *Chabad.org/1814200*.
- Eating matzah on the day before Passover undermines the whole story. So that's a no-no even for children, as long as they are old enough to have some idea of what's going on. Many refrain from eating matzah an entire month before Passover.

Matzah

The Edible Mitzvah

Matzah is more than a food, it's the way we relive the Exodus. It's also the only Biblical mitzvah we have today that we actually eat and digest. According to Kabbalah, the matzah you eat on the first night of Passover strengthens the faith of the soul, and matzah eaten on the second night heals both body and soul. So make sure you **get the real thing** because not all matzah is created equal. There's…

YEAR-ROUND MATZAH

Looks like matzah, tastes like matzah, and has the same ingredients as matzah—but it wasn't made for Passover, and so no one made sure that it did not become chametz, which is forbidden on Passover.

Not kosher for Passover under any conditions.

"RICH" MATZAH

Matzah made with fruit juice, eggs, or some other extra ingredients.

This matzah shouldn't be used for the Seder.

If certified kosher for Passover, the Ashkenazic custom is that it may be used after the Seder, during the rest of Passover, only by the ill, or those who (for health reasons) simply cannot stomach plain matzah. The Sephardic custom is varied.

 Read more about this at Chabad.org/1163475.

MACHINE-MADE SHMURAH MATZAH

Matzah that was carefully guarded from all moisture from the moment it was harvested all the way until it reached your Seder table.

Almost the ultimate matzah, but not ideal for the Seder.

PESACH OFFERING

אֵינָם דּוֹחִין אֶת הַשַּׁבָּת. וְכֵן אֵין מוֹלִיכִין אֶת הַפֶּסַח לַבַּיִת כְּשֶׁחָל בְּשַׁבָּת, אֶלָּא כַּת הָאַחַת הֵם מִתְעַכְּבִים עִם פִּסְחֵיהֶם בְּהַר הַבַּיִת, וְהַכַּת הַשְּׁנִיָּה יוֹשֶׁבֶת לָהּ בַּחֵיל, וְהַשְּׁלִישִׁית בִּמְקוֹמָהּ עוֹמֶדֶת. חָשְׁכָה, יָצְאוּ וְצָלוּ פִּסְחֵיהֶם. בִּשְׁלֹשָׁה כִּתּוֹת הַפֶּסַח נִשְׁחָט, וְאֵין כַּת פְּחוּתָה מִשְּׁלֹשִׁים אֲנָשִׁים. נִכְנְסָה כַּת הָרִאשׁוֹנָה, נִתְמַלְּאָה הָעֲזָרָה, נוֹעֲלִין אוֹתָהּ. וּבְעוֹד שֶׁהֵם שׁוֹחֲטִין וּמַקְרִיבִין אֶת הָאֵמוּרִים, קוֹרְאִין אֶת הַהַלֵּל. אִם גָּמְרוּ אוֹתוֹ קוֹדֶם שֶׁיַּקְרִיבוּ כֻלָּם, שׁוֹנִים אוֹתוֹ, וְאִם שָׁנוּ יְשַׁלֵּשׁוּ. עַל כָּל קְרִיאָה תּוֹקְעִין שָׁלֹשׁ תְּקִיעוֹת: תְּקִיעָה תְּרוּעָה תְּקִיעָה. גָּמְרוּ לְהַקְרִיב, פּוֹתְחִין הָעֲזָרָה. יָצְאָה כַּת רִאשׁוֹנָה, נִכְנְסָה כַּת שְׁנִיָּה, נוֹעֲלִין דַּלְתוֹת הָעֲזָרָה. גָּמְרוּ, פּוֹתְחִין. יָצְאָה כַּת שְׁנִיָּה, נִכְנְסָה כַּת שְׁלִישִׁית, וּמַעֲשֵׂה כֻלָּן שָׁוִין. וְאַחַר שֶׁיָּצְאוּ כֻלָּן רוֹחֲצִין הָעֲזָרָה, וַאֲפִלּוּ בְּשַׁבָּת, מִפְּנֵי לִכְלוּךְ הַדָּם שֶׁהָיָה בָּהּ. וְכֵיצַד הָיְתָה הָרְחִיצָה? אַמַּת הַמַּיִם הָיְתָה עוֹבֶרֶת בָּעֲזָרָה, וְהָיָה לָהּ מָקוֹם לָצֵאת מִמֶּנָּה, וּכְשֶׁרוֹצִין לְהָדִיחַ אֶת הָרִצְפָּה, סוֹתְמִין מְקוֹם יְצִיאָתָהּ, וְהִיא מִתְמַלֵּאת עַל כָּל גְּדוֹתֶיהָ מִפֹּה וּמִפֹּה, עַד שֶׁהַמַּיִם עוֹלִים וְצָפִים מִכָּאן וּמִכָּאן, וּמְקַבֵּץ אֵלֶיהָ כָּל דָּם וְכָל לִכְלוּךְ שֶׁהָיָה בָעֲזָרָה. וְאַחַר כָּךְ פּוֹתְחִין מְקוֹם יְצִיאָתָהּ, וְהַכֹּל יוֹצֵא עַד שֶׁנִּשְׁאָר הָרִצְפָּה מְנֻקָּה וּמְשֻׁפָּה. זֶהוּ כְּבוֹד הַבַּיִת. וְאִם הַפֶּסַח נִמְצָא טְרֵפָה, לֹא עָלָה לוֹ עַד שֶׁיָּבִיא אַחֵר:

The slaughtering, the sprinkling of its blood, the cleansing of its bowels, and the burning of its fat override the Shabbat. But anything else done with it does not.

Likewise, if the fourteenth of Nissan occurs on Shabbat, the Pesach offerings can't be carried home. Instead, one group remains with their Pesach offerings on the Temple mount outside the Temple courtyard, the second group sits in the *chel* (an intermediate area just outside the Temple court), and the third stands in its place in the Temple courtyard. They wait there until after nightfall, when everyone goes to their places and roasts their Pesach offering.

The Pesach offering was slaughtered in three groups, each consisting of no less than thirty men.

The first group entered, filling the Temple court, and they closed the doors.

While they were slaughtering the offerings and bringing their parts onto the altar, they (principally the Levi'im) recited the Hallel. If they finished Hallel before all had made their offerings, they repeated it, and if the people were still not done, they recited it a third time.

Each time Hallel was recited, the kohanim sounded three blasts of the trumpet: tekiah, teruah, tekiah.

When all the offerings were done, they opened the doors of the Temple court. The first group left, the second entered, and they closed the doors of the Temple court.

When that group finished, they opened the doors again so that the second group left and the third entered.

The procedure with each group was the same.

Then, after all three groups left, they washed the Temple court—even on Shabbat—of the mess of blood.

How was the washing done?

A stream of water passed through the Temple court. It had an outlet from the court. When they wished to wash the floor, they shut that outlet and the stream overflowed its sides, until the water rose and flooded the floor all around and gathered all the blood and refuse of the court. They then opened the outlet, everything flowed out, and the floor was completely clean. This was all to keep the honor of the Temple.

If the Pesach offering you bring is found to be unkosher, you haven't fulfilled your obligation until you bring another one.

For most of us, it's difficult to visualize ourselves involved in bringing this offering. But then, it's also difficult to imagine the dramatic shift in global events that must occur for the messianic times of peace and wisdom to dawn upon the world.

Yet, it could all happen overnight. And once that occurs and we experience the spiritual high of entering the Temple courtyard, then everything we have just read will make perfect sense.

Order of the Pesach Offering

As we went to print with this edition, Moshiach had not yet arrived and the necessary conditions for bringing a Pesach offering were still lacking. Under such circumstances, the custom is to study out loud the order and rules for this offering at the time when it was brought, namely, the afternoon before the Seder night. So we say this immediately after the Mincha prayer.

There are three planes upon which you can do any mitzvah: You can think about it, you can speak about it, and you can do it. Of course, doing it is the most important, but what if you can't? You can still be engaged in the holiness and divine beauty of the mitzvah by immersing your mind in its thought-dimension and filling your mouth with its words.

קָרְבַּן פֶּסַח מֵבִיא מִן הַכְּבָשִׂים אוֹ מִן הָעִזִּים זָכָר בֶּן שָׁנָה, וְשׁוֹחֲטוֹ בָּעֲזָרָה בְּכָל מָקוֹם, אַחַר חֲצוֹת אַרְבָּעָה עָשָׂר דַּוְקָא, וְאַחַר שְׁחִיטַת תָּמִיד שֶׁל בֵּין הָעַרְבַּיִם, וְאַחַר הֲטָבַת נֵרוֹת שֶׁל בֵּין הָעַרְבַּיִם. וְאֵין שׁוֹחֲטִין אֶת הַפֶּסַח עַל הֶחָמֵץ. וְאִם שָׁחַט קוֹדֶם לַתָּמִיד, כָּשֵׁר, וּבִלְבַד שֶׁיְּהֵא אַחֵר מְמָרֵס בְּדַם הַפֶּסַח כְּדֵי שֶׁלֹּא יִקְרֹשׁ עַד שֶׁיִּזְרְקוּ דַם הַתָּמִיד, וְאַחַר כָּךְ יִזְרְקוּ דַם הַפֶּסַח זְרִיקָה אַחַת כְּנֶגֶד הַיְסוֹד. וְכֵיצַד עוֹשִׂין? שָׁחַט הַשּׁוֹחֵט, וְקִבֵּל הַכֹּהֵן הָרִאשׁוֹן שֶׁבָּרֹאשׁ הַשּׁוּרָה וְנָתַן לַחֲבֵרוֹ, וַחֲבֵרוֹ לַחֲבֵרוֹ, וְהַכֹּהֵן הַקָּרוֹב אֵצֶל הַמִּזְבֵּחַ זוֹרְקוֹ זְרִיקָה אַחַת כְּנֶגֶד הַיְסוֹד, וְחוֹזֵר הַכְּלִי רֵיקָן לַחֲבֵרוֹ, וַחֲבֵרוֹ לַחֲבֵרוֹ, וּמְקַבֵּל כְּלִי הַמָּלֵא תְּחִלָּה וְאַחַר כָּךְ מַחֲזִיר הָרֵיקָן. וְהָיוּ שׁוּרוֹת שֶׁל בָּזִיכֵי כֶּסֶף וְשׁוּרוֹת שֶׁל בָּזִיכֵי זָהָב. וְלֹא הָיוּ לַבָּזִיכִין שׁוּלַיִם, שֶׁמָּא יַנִּיחֵם וְיִקְרֹשׁ הַדָּם. אַחַר כָּךְ תּוֹלִין אֶת הַפֶּסַח וּמַפְשִׁיטִין אוֹתוֹ כֻּלּוֹ, וְקוֹרְעִין אוֹתוֹ, וּמְמַחִין אֶת קְרָבָיו עַד שֶׁיֵּצֵא הַפֶּרֶשׁ, וּמוֹצִיאִין אֶת הָאֵימוּרִים, וְהֵם: הַחֵלֶב שֶׁעַל הַקֶּרֶב, וְיוֹתֶרֶת הַכָּבֵד, וּשְׁתֵּי כְלָיוֹת וְהַחֵלֶב שֶׁעֲלֵיהֶן, וְהָאַלְיָה לְעֻמַּת הָעָצֶה, וְנוֹתְנָם בִּכְלִי שָׁרֵת, וּמוֹלְחָם וּמַקְטִירָם הַכֹּהֵן עַל גַּבֵּי הַמִּזְבֵּחַ כָּל אֶחָד לְבַדּוֹ. וְהַשְּׁחִיטָה וְהַזְּרִיקָה וּמִחוּי קְרָבָיו וְהֶקְטֵר חֲלָבָיו דּוֹחִין אֶת הַשַּׁבָּת, וּשְׁאָר עִנְיָנָיו

FOR a Pesach offering, you can bring a lamb or a goat, male and in its first year.

It could be slaughtered anywhere in the Temple court, but only after midday of the fourteenth of Nissan. It also had to be after the slaughtering of the daily afternoon offering, and after the afternoon cleaning of the cups of the menorah.

It's forbidden to slaughter the Pesach offering as long as you have chametz in your possession.

If, however, you slaughtered it before the daily afternoon offering, it is still acceptable—as long as you have someone stir the blood of this offering so that it doesn't congeal before the blood of the daily afternoon offering is sprinkled.

Next, the blood of that Pesach offering needs to be sprinkled once toward the base of the altar. How was that done?

Kohanim formed lines from the slaughtering area to the altar. As soon as someone slaughtered the animal, the kohen at the head of the line collected its blood as it poured into a container. He handed that over to the next in line, and that kohen to the next, and so on, until the kohen nearest the altar sprinkled it once toward the base of the altar.

That kohen then returned the empty container to the one before him, and that kohen to the next, and so on. Each kohen was continually receiving full containers and passing back empty ones, always making sure to receive a full one before passing back the empty one.

There were rows of silver containers and rows of golden containers. To prevent the blood from congealing if it was still for too long, none of them had flat bottoms.

Next, they hung the Pesach offering, flayed it completely, tore it open, and cleansed its bowels until all the waste came out.

They then took out the parts offered on the altar—the fat on the entrails, the lobe of the liver, the two kidneys with the fat on them, and the tail up to the backbone—and placed them in a ritual container.

A kohen then salted them and burned them upon the altar, each one individually.

After throwing your chametz in the fire,* make the following declaration:

כָּל חֲמִירָא וַחֲמִיעָא דְּאִכָּא בִרְשׁוּתִי, דַּחֲזִיתֵיהּ וּדְלָא חֲזִיתֵיהּ, דַּחֲמִיתֵיהּ וּדְלָא חֲמִיתֵיהּ, דְּבִעַרְתֵּיהּ וּדְלָא בִעַרְתֵּיהּ, לִבָּטֵל וְלֶהֱוֵי הֶפְקֵר כְּעַפְרָא דְאַרְעָא:

ALL leaven and anything leavened that is in my possession—whether I have seen it or not, whether I have observed it or not, whether I have removed it or not—shall be considered naught and ownerless as the dust of the earth.

You are now chametz-free—and free to enjoy the liberating Seder experience and the Festival of Freedom.

While the chametz is burning,** say this chametz-burning meditation/prayer:

יְהִי רָצוֹן מִלְּפָנֶיךָ יְיָ אֱלֹהֵינוּ וֵאלֹהֵי אֲבוֹתֵינוּ, כְּשֵׁם שֶׁאֲנִי מְבַעֵר חָמֵץ מִבֵּיתִי וּמֵרְשׁוּתִי, כָּךְ תְּבַעֵר אֶת כָּל הַחִיצוֹנִים, וְאֶת רוּחַ הַטֻּמְאָה תַּעֲבִיר מִן הָאָרֶץ, וְאֶת יִצְרֵנוּ הָרַע תַּעֲבִירֵהוּ מֵאִתָּנוּ, וְתִתֶּן לָנוּ לֵב בָּשָׂר לְעָבְדְּךָ בֶּאֱמֶת, וְכָל סִטְרָא אַחֲרָא וְכָל הַקְּלִפּוֹת וְכָל הָרִשְׁעָה בֶּעָשָׁן תִּכְלֶה, וְתַעֲבִיר מֶמְשֶׁלֶת זָדוֹן מִן הָאָרֶץ, וְכָל הַמְּעִיקִים לַשְּׁכִינָה תְּבַעֲרֵם בְּרוּחַ בָּעֵר וּבְרוּחַ מִשְׁפָּט כְּשֵׁם שֶׁבִּעַרְתָּ אֶת מִצְרַיִם וְאֶת אֱלֹהֵיהֶם בַּיָּמִים הָהֵם בַּזְּמַן הַזֶּה, אָמֵן סֶלָה:

LET a new desire emerge from within You, God, our God and God of our fathers, that just as I have eradicated chametz from my home and from my possession, so You will eradicate all the forces of evil from Your world and obliterate the spirit of impurity from the earth.

Eliminate our wicked impulses from within us and give us a heart of flesh so we may truly serve You.

May all the Side of Otherness ("sitra achra"), and all the thick disguises that conceal the divine life within them ("kelipot"), along with all wickedness, go up in smoke as You vanquish the dominance of evil from the earth.

And all the oppressors of the Shechinah—may You obliterate them with a spirit of vanquishment and a spirit of justice just as You vanquished Ancient Egypt and its deities in those days at this time.

Amen, Selah!

---

* Or disposing of it on Shabbat, when Passover begins on Saturday night.

** On years when Passover begins on Saturday night, make sure you say the second "Kol Chamira"—"All leaven..." declaration (printed above) on Shabbat morning, after disposing of the remains of the chametz that you've eaten.

After nightfall, gather the family, light a candle, and say:

בָּרוּךְ אַתָּה יְיָ אֱלֹהֵינוּ מֶלֶךְ הָעוֹלָם, אֲשֶׁר קִדְּשָׁנוּ בְּמִצְוֹתָיו, וְצִוָּנוּ עַל בִּעוּר חָמֵץ:

(Listeners: אָמֵן)

BLESSED are You, God, our God, King of the universe, who has made us holy with His mitzvahs, and commanded us regarding the removal of chametz.

(Listeners: **Amen**)

- Thoroughly search your home and car for any chametz.
- Bag the evidence and store it away for tomorrow's chametz-burning ceremony.
- After the search, make the following declaration:

כָּל חֲמִירָא וַחֲמִיעָא דְּאִכָּא בִרְשׁוּתִי, דְּלָא חֲמִיתֵיהּ וּדְלָא בִעַרְתֵּיהּ וּדְלָא יְדַעְנָא לֵיהּ, לִבָּטֵל וְלֶהֱוֵי הֶפְקֵר כְּעַפְרָא דְאַרְעָא:

ALL leaven and anything leavened that is in my possession—which I have neither seen nor removed, and about which I am unaware—shall be considered naught and ownerless as the dust of the earth.

The Day Before Passover*

Like we said earlier, on Passover, it's not just that we don't eat chametz, we mustn't even own it.

Well, now is the last chance to sell your chametz! Make sure to do it before the time limit for chametz-burning.

You can still eat chametz for breakfast, as long as you finish before the **chametz-eating time limit.** After that, eat only kosher-for-Passover foods.

Before the **chametz-burning time limit,** make a fire and burn the chametz bag from last night, plus any other leftover chametz that hasn't been sold.

 To find your local chametz-eating and chametz-burning time limits, visit Chabad.org/PassoverTimes.

---

* What if it's one of those years (like 2025 and 2045) **when the day before Passover is Shabbat**—which means you're doing all this on Friday? You can eat chametz until Saturday morning, but you should sell your chametz and burn that bag on Friday before the chametz-burning time limit. Then, on Saturday morning, you'll need to eat and dispose of any remaining chametz by the cut-off time listed for that day. Make sure you check for that time before Shabbat.

Best way to dispose of chametz on Shabbat is to crumble it up and flush it down the toilet. If you just toss it in the trash, it's still in your possession.

 For more details on this Shabbat situation, see Chabad.org/5025853.

The Chametz Search-and-Destroy Mission

The Night Before Passover*

Once the house is Passover-tidy, it's time to do the search-and-destroy ritual.

Here's a mitzvah that kids love to be part of and that will stay with them forever. Before the search, carefully wrap ten pieces of bread in paper and hide them throughout the house. Keep a list of where you hid them (your smartphone's camera comes in handy here).

Search your home for the chametz with a lighted candle. Aside from the candle, the custom is to take along a feather, a wooden spoon and a paper bag (all to be burned later with the chametz). The feather is meant for sweeping any chametz you might find into the bag. The spoon is to stick in the bag (with the handle sticking out) when you tie it all up, to help it all burn.

Away from home for the holiday? Ask your rabbi when and how to do the search.

---

* Or the night before that. In some years (such as 2025 and 2045), the day before Passover is Shabbat. In that case, you'll need to follow these instructions on Thursday night and Friday morning.

The Sellout

Now you're thinking, "What about my 30-year single-malt whiskey and my kid's Cheerio-Man masterpiece?" For these items and anything else you don't want to dispose of, there's an alternative: Simply ensure that they do not belong to you during Passover. Here's how:

1. Gather all the chametz you want to save—food, drinks, and any utensils that might still have food stuck to them.
2. Store it all away in a closet or room.
3. Lock the area or tape it shut.
4. Clean utensils don't need to be locked up with all the chametz. Just keep them closeted off from your Passover utensils, so they won't be used by mistake.
5. Authorize an experienced rabbi to make a legally binding sale according to both Jewish and civil law.

> Visit Chabad.org/Chametz to do this online.

The rabbi will sell all your chametz just before Passover and buy it back as soon as the holiday is over. The night Passover ends, after the rabbi has purchased back your chametz, you can already break out that single malt for a *l'chaim*.

WHAT'S SO TERRIBLE about chametz? After all, we eat it the whole year long, no problem.

And if it's just a commemoration of leaving Egypt, why the concern over less than a crumb?

In fact, Rabbi Isaac Luria, the 16th-century master kabbalist, known as the Arizal, taught that if you're careful to avoid consuming even the smallest amount of chametz on Passover, God will protect you from committing any misdeeds the entire year.

But why? What's the connection?

Well, it's like Rabbi Alexandri says in the Talmud (Berachot 17a):

"Master of the Universe! It's obvious to You that we want to do what You want done. So what is holding us back? It's the sourdough that makes the bread rise!"

You see, a little bit of chametz makes a little dough into a big loaf of hot air. And that pretty much describes the fundamental gameplay of all that imprisons all of us.

Like the chametz that takes your healthy need to earn an honest living and blows it up into a desperate need for recognition and yet more recognition.

Or like the chametz that mixes in when you are about to do a beautiful mitzvah out of the sincerity of your heart, saying, "Yes! Do it! People will say you are such a tzadik!"

Or the chametz that appears when you are studying the wisdom of Torah and whispers, "Soon you will be wiser than anyone else!"

It's that chametz that ties every thought, every word, every deed you do to your ego, as though your existence is somehow invalidated if you do not occupy more and more space every day—with nothing but hot air.

We are its prisoner. It is our taskmaster. It has stolen our lives from us, rendering us all subjects of an oppressive world we must satisfy and please.

On Passover we are empowered to break our chains of bondage. To do a mitzvah only because it connects us to our God. To learn Torah wisdom only to become one with divine wisdom. To be ourselves. To escape bondage to anything in this world. To be free.

And we begin by eradicating a physical manifestation of that ego from our world. Torah provides a powerful tool: Just by temporarily eliminating chametz from our lives, we can set ourselves free.

Passover Preparations

Who is this chametz guy, and how do I get rid of him?

Chametz means "leavened grain." On Passover, it's not just that we don't eat chametz, we mustn't even own it.

Here's a simple rule of thumb: If a food or drink contains even a trace of wheat, barley, rye, oats, spelt, or their derivatives, and wasn't guarded against leavening or fermentation—it's chametz. Which means that any processed food or drink today can be assumed to be chametz unless certified otherwise.

Problem is, our homes are full of this stuff. That's why we go on a full cleaning and search-and-destroy mission during the weeks before Passover.

Here's how:

Target any and all areas where food may enter (you don't have to bother with places where food never comes). Move the furniture, oven and fridge. Search beneath the sofa cushions and clean out whatever other hard-to-reach places that are reachable. Wipe chairs, cupboards and bookshelves clean.

Don't forget your office. Even if you don't own your office, you own any food you keep there. Plus any lockers or storage places you use at work or at school. Check the pockets of clothing in the closet. And then, of course, there's that mobile snack bar of yours, the car.

The prime target, of course, is the kitchen. After cleaning it, you can use foil or paper to line all surfaces that may come in contact with food. You can also run the self-clean cycle on your oven, if it supports it.

You'll want separate utensils and appliances for Passover use. If this is not possible, some kitchen items can be made kosher for Passover.

See Chabad.org/117233 for more on this.

How to Use This Haggadah

Use this Haggadah however you like, adding your own family customs, fitting it to your particular situation. But here are a few suggestions that can help your Seder really take off:

- First off, a no-brainer: Go around the table and give everyone a chance to read. Simple—and it works. We've even marked suggested places to switch off readers with these icons:

- But you still need to use those brains. Pace yourself. Determine how much time you have, and keep things moving so that you can get through everything without having to rush anything.

- If you want to go all the way, divide up roles. One person for each of the four children. Someone else to be the parent. Choose someone to be Rabbi Eliezer. Someone else can be Ben Zoma. Go through the Haggadah in advance and see how it can work out. Or just work it out on the fly.

- In some communities, everyone reads every word of the Haggadah in Hebrew. If you want to go all the way, try this: Each time you're about to switch readers, have everyone read the Hebrew together first.

- Want to make someone feel real important? Appoint someone as "instruction reader."

- And while we're thinking ahead already: Ask each person who is invited to your Seder to prepare something short to say or explain at the Seder. Tell them they can research everything online beforehand.

- For a real wild and wonderful Seder, watch "How to Make a Wild & Wonderful Passover Seder" at *Chabad.org/1156813*. You'll find there a list of props that you'll want to get before Passover, and other printouts that will come in handy. After watching, go through this Haggadah and pencil in your itinerary.

This icon denotes an additional pearl of wisdom. Have someone share this insight from our sages.

 This icon denotes a link to access more information before the holiday.

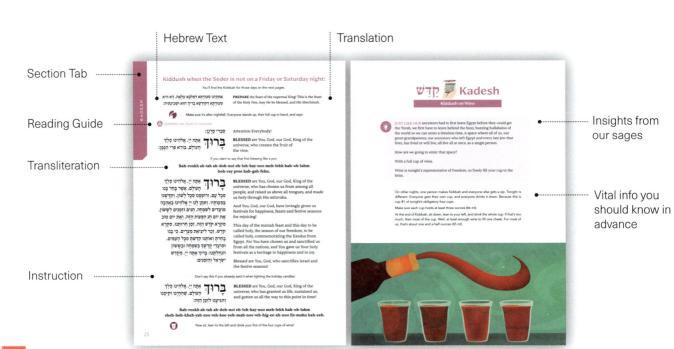

The Haggadah

This Is Not an Introduction

Here's some stuff you gotta read.
Crucial to understand this Haggadah.

Yes, it's a traditional Haggadah. It follows all the standard texts and commentaries from the whole gamut of Jewish history, like a thousand voices harmonized into a single symphony.

But that's the thing about the traditional Haggadah: You'll find everything in there—except your own voice. That you have to add yourself.

And that's vital. Because, as the Haggadah says, you have to tell this story as though it happened to you. Because, in truth, it is a story that happens to each one of us in our lives.

Which is where this particular Haggadah comes in. We haven't changed the traditional Haggadah. We've just made it easier to find yourself there.

You see, instead of simply translating the words, we followed an ancient Jewish tradition called *targum*. That's when a translation lays all the context, implications and backstage story out in the open, in clear, simple language.

We also made sure to use modern language and idioms. And we did it in a way that should prove fun for all.

Our goal was to simulate as best we could a Seder which you, your family, and friends might have improvised organically, as though the classic Haggadah of our ancestors was flowing naturally through your souls, minds and mouths.

The Seder table is a timeless space.

The Haggadah contains the story that creates that space.

With this Haggadah, you will bring that timelessness to your table and into your home.

"In every generation each Jew should see himself as though he personally had been liberated from Egypt."

of the greatest plague), and Matzah—then the very catastrophe and the enemies of the Jews will work for the benefit of the Jews, driving them in great haste out of "Mitzraim" [Egypt], the place of perversion and darkness, and placing them under the beam of light and holiness.

One other important thing we must remember. The celebration of the festival of freedom must be connected with the commandment "You shall relate it to your son." The formation and existence of the Jewish home, as of the Jewish people as a whole, is dependent upon the upbringing of the young generation, both boys and girls: the wise and the wicked (temporarily), the simple and the one who knows not what to ask. Just as we cannot shirk our responsibility towards our child by the excuse that "my child is a wise one; he will find his own way in life, therefore no education is necessary for him"; so we must not despair by thinking "the child is a wicked one; no education will help him." For all Jewish children, boys and girls, are "G-d's children," and it is our sacred duty to see to it that they all live up to their above-mentioned title; and this we can achieve only through a kosher Jewish education, in full adherence to G-d's Torah. Then we all will merit the realization of our ardent hopes: "In the next year may we be free; in the next year may we be in Jerusalem!¹"

—Rabbi Menachem M. Schneerson

A Passover Message From the Rebbe
Rabbi Menachem M. Schneerson, of righteous memory

The festival of Passover calls for early and elaborate preparations to make the Jewish home fitting for the great festival. It is not physical preparedness alone that is required of us, but also spiritual preparedness—for in the life of the Jew the physical and spiritual are closely linked together, especially in the celebration of our Sabbath and festivals.

On Passover we celebrate the liberation of the Jewish people from Egyptian slavery and, together with it, the liberation from, and negation of, the ancient Egyptian system and way of life, the "abominations of Egypt." Thus we celebrate our physical liberation together with our spiritual freedom. Indeed, there cannot be one without the other; there can be no real freedom without accepting the precepts of our Torah guiding our daily life; pure and holy life eventually leads to real freedom.

It is said: "In every generation each Jew should see himself as though he personally had been liberated from Egypt." This is to say that the lesson of Passover has *always* a timely message for the individual Jew. The story of Passover is the story of the special Divine Providence which alone determines the fate of our people. What is happening in the outside world need not affect us; we might be singled out for suffering, G-d forbid, amid general prosperity, and likewise singled out for safety amid a general plague or catastrophe. The story of our enslavement and liberation, of which Passover tells us, give ample illustration of this. For the fate of our people is determined by its adherence to G-d and His Prophets.

This lesson is emphasized by the three principal symbols of the Seder, concerning which our Sages said that unless the Jew explains their significance he has not observed the Seder fittingly: Pesach [the Paschal Offering], Matzah and Maror [bitter herbs]. Using these symbols in their chronological order and in accordance with the Haggadah explanation, we may say: the Jew can avoid Maror (bitterness of life) only through Pesach (G-d's special care 'passing over' and saving the Jewish homes even in the midst

ב"ה

Table of Contents

A Passover Message 4
Introduction 6
How to Use This Haggadah 7

Preparing for Passover

Getting Rid of Chametz 8
Order of the Pesach Offering 14
Matzah 16
Pre-Passover Shopping List 18
What You'll Need for the Seder 19
Candle Lighting 20

The Seder

Setting Up the Seder Plate 21
Tonight's Program 22
Kadesh • Kiddush on Wine 24
Urchatz • Wash Hands, No Blessing 30
Karpas • Eat a Vegetable in Salt Water 30
Yachatz • Break a Matzah 31
Magid • Tell the Story 32
Rachtza • Wash Hands with a Blessing 70
Motzi • Blessing on the Matzah 71
Matzah • Blessing on the Mitzvah 71
Maror • Bitter Leaves for Eating 72
Korech • Bitter Leaves in a Wrapping 73
Shulchan Orech • A Festive Meal 74
Tzafun • Eat the Afikoman 74
Beirach • Thank God for the Meal 75
Hallel-Nirtzah • Praise God 86

Appendix

Shalom Aleichem & Eshet Chayil 104
Kiddush for Daytime 107
Hamotzi 110
Sources 111

The Chabad.org Haggadah

Third Edition

© Copyright 2023 by Chabad.org, all rights reserved.

Created by
Chabad.org
788 Eastern Parkway, Suite 405, Brooklyn NY 11213

Published by
Kehot Publication Society
770 Eastern Parkway, Brooklyn NY 11213

Concept & Targum	Rabbi Tzvi Freeman
Executive Editor	Rabbi Meir Simcha Kogan
Creative Director	Rabbi Motti Seligson
Executive Director	Rabbi Zalman Shmotkin
Cover & Illustrations	Sefira Lightstone © sefiracreative.com
Layout & Design	Racheli Chazan, Shneor Cortez, Sholom Ber Gurary and Spotlight Design
Rabbinic Review	Rabbi Avrohom Altein and Rabbi Levi Friedman
Editorial Team	Rabbi Simcha Bart, Chani Benjaminson, Rabbi Avi Eskinazi, Rabbi Alex Heppenheimer, Rabbi Mendy Kaminker, Yaakov Ort, Rabbi Menachem Posner and Rabbi Yehuda Shurpin
Hebrew Text	Hebrew text of the Haggadah is copyright Kehot Publication Society and is used with permission.

We hope you enjoy this Haggadah and that it enhances your Passover Seder. Please share your feedback and suggestions with us at feedback@chabad.org.

All rights reserved. No part of this publication may be reproduced, stored in a retrieval system, or transmitted in any form or by any means, electronic, mechanical, photocopying, recording, or otherwise, without prior permission from the copyright holder.

ISBN 978-0-8266-0627-3 (hardcover)
978-0-8266-0628-0 (paperback)

4 6 8 10 12 13 11 9 7 5

The publication contains sacred literature. Please do not deface or discard.

The Chabad.org Haggadah
הגדה של פסח

For a meaningful, fun and uplifting Passover Seder